Writing into the Sunset

Starting Your Writing Career After Retirement

John A. Bredesen

Kennd Publishing
North St. Paul, MN
kennd-publishing.com

Copyright © 2022 John A. Bredesen. johnbredesen.com johnbredesen.com
All rights reserved. For questions about reproducing selections from this book or quantity purchases, email info@kennd-publishing.com.

ISBN 978-1-7366500-9-7

Editor: Kristin Erlandsen
Cover : Dex Greenbright
Fonts: Adobe Garamond Pro & Chaparral Pro

Publisher's Notes:
- Web sites used as links or references may change after publication.
- Search terms will return results that change over time. The publisher and author expect the reader to use good judgment to choose appropriate results to learn the concepts.
- Advice provided in this book may not be appropriate in your situation. Good judgment is required when applying any advice received from a book.

Contents

Introduction	1
Chapter 1: My Story	7
Chapter 2: Benefits of Being Retirement Age	17
Chapter 3: Your Opponent	25
Chapter 4: The Journey	43
Chapter 5: Writing Non-Fiction	73
Chapter 6: Writing Fiction	83
Chapter 7: The Tools	99
Chapter 8: The Business	109
Summary	135
Resources	139

Dedication

To Mrs. V, one of my high school English teachers.

Mrs. V, thanks for the lessons about the meanings behind the words. You taught me that the world of words was as rich and deep as my imagination.

Introduction

***"You can't retire FROM something.
You have to retire TO something."***

Marge jabbed her finger at me with each word, like a lawyer making a point during closing arguments. Her husband, Dick, chimed in with her last few words, creating a chorus of well-meaning chastisement.

I was chatting with this delightful couple after church one sunny spring morning. We were talking about their retirement travels and how great retirement was. I made a comment something like "I don't see myself retiring for a long time. I don't know what I would do with myself." I was in my mid-50s and retirement seemed like a long way off.

Cue the jabbing.

"You can't retire FROM something, you have to retire TO something."

Those words stuck with me. I had seen others retire and had seen different approaches. Some people got real active, some people practically disappeared. Some people went back to work. I couldn't just stop doing what I had been doing. Besides, I enjoyed my work. I needed something to retire to.

I ended up deciding to be a writer. In order to make the transition, I had to learn a lot. There are lots of books, websites, and podcasts about making a career out of writing (overly simplified summary: don't quit your day job). One thing I couldn't find, however, was information targeted at people who were writing in their retirement years. I felt that retirement gave me an advantage, but I wasn't seeing it in the books.

Writing is the only skill I can think of where you use the specific skill to teach others to do that skill. You can't teach computers by only writing software, you can't teach painting by only painting, and you can't teach baseball by only playing. Those teaching those skills always resort to words to explain how to get better. And words? Well, that is the writer's stock in trade.

One side effect of this phenomenon is that there are a lot of books and articles written by writers to help others learn to be better writers or how to sell more books or how to get better at ads. Books with writing advice have become more common than squirrels around a bird feeder. As you might expect, the quality and usefulness of these books varies widely.

Yet, here I am writing another writing book. Focused on writing after retirement.

When I started outlining this book, I was still planning on retirement in the future. I figure the first edition of the book would cover what I did to get started and to prepare for retirement. Unfortunately, life doesn't always work out the way you expect and I retired earlier than planned.

So here is my third book. I drew from my long IT career and wrote two non-fiction books aimed at IT leaders. I focused this book on becoming a writer in your retirement. I wrote it to capture the things I learned as I prepared for and then started a retirement of writing.

The change to retirement life can be hard. There is a transition from a schedule set by work to a schedule set by you. There may be financial adjustments to make. Working took most of your waking hours and now that demand on your time is gone. Writing will take up some of your time, but maybe you don't want it to become another full-time job.

The journey to becoming a writer has many paths, most of them dependent on you. None of these paths are wrong. Unfortunately, you won't find your path written neatly in a book, even this one. Setting out on this journey will require a leap of faith. Don't worry if the path you initially choose doesn't work out. You can always change and try something different.

As I will cover in the book, knowing why you are writing is important. Don't worry, there are no wrong reasons. My reasons are to write and sell books. I have loved books since I discovered my parents' bookshelves in my early teens. I also enjoy business, so learning about how to market and sell books interests me.

Your reasons will be different. That's great. You need to be you. Hopefully, you will pick up a few things from this book that will help you understand why you want to write.

Being our age has several benefits that are helpful to understand. We have years of experience at life. We have a different perspective than we did when we were young. We have a better sense of how our internal self works.

All of this works in our favor.

About This Book

I wrote this book with the idea that you can either read straight through or skip around. There is a table of contents and an index to help you find specific topics.

The term "retirement age" means the set of years from when we seriously start thinking about retirement through the first few years of retirement. This can be a wide range of ages.

Everyone has different opportunities, challenges, and experiences. We all made different decisions to deal with whatever life threw at us. Some of what I write in this book won't match your experiences. That is a fact. But I tried to use those experiences to make larger points that hopefully will fit your situation. An example is kids: I have kids, many don't. Both are valid experiences. So keep an eye on the larger point and don't pay too much attention to my specifics—they aren't important to your journey.

There are a couple of beliefs I have that influence my approach to writing.

- We can learn almost anything with time and the right attitude.

- We can break bad habits and create new habits with time and the right attitude. Conversely, each of us has habits we haven't (so far) been able to start or break.

- Trying things and failing is an important part of learning. If you aren't failing, you aren't learning. For example, read about how Stephen King dealt with rejection letters. See the "Resources" chapter at the end of the book for more information.

- Everyone is creative. A lifetime of being part of society has caused many of us to wall off our creativity. Much of the hard work of writing is breaking down those walls.

- We all think our writing is terrible. Sometimes we are right, sometimes we aren't.

- I am a believer in the 10,000-hours theory. This theory, popularized by Malcolm Gladwell in his book *Outliers*, puts forth the idea that you must put in 10,000 hours of good practice to excel in any field. I don't buy the specific number, it could be more or less, but the concept is absolutely correct: We can't excel at something unless we put in the time.

- I also am a believer in "as you practice, so shall you play." Practice sloppy, play sloppy. Practice correctly, play correctly. Learning how to do something right and then practicing the right way, makes all the difference. Those of you familiar with the concept of deliberate practice know what I am talking about.

- Except for the Introduction, each chapter starts with a Haiku. There is no good reason for it other than, hey, I got to write poetry and it was fun. One of my take-aways from my journey is that you need to enjoy the writing process. It won't always be puppies and chocolates, but if you don't enjoy the process, the hard work needed will wear you down faster than a young grandkid asking questions.

One last point before we get started here. I wrote this book to collect my thoughts on writing. I don't have all this figured out; I don't have any guarantee of success. Some of what I learned will be helpful to you, but you do you regardless of what anyone says.

Let's dive in and get started!

Chapter 1: My Story

Ahead, the sunset
Behind me, the career ends
Creating is now

When my high school English teacher had me stay late after class one day, my 15-year-old self knew it wasn't good news. I watched the other kids leaving, glancing back at me in pity, as I slowly walked up to the front of the room.

Her actual words are long lost in the fog of memory. All I remember was she had called my parents in for a quick chat at the end of the school day to talk about my disappointing grades.

Great. Just great.

When the time came, I sat at a desk about halfway across the room from the teacher. My parents sat a few feet away from her. We were in a strange circle, all facing each other, with three points close together and me as far away as I could get.

As my teacher talked through my abysmal English grades, I stared at the floor, glancing at my parents once in a while to see how they were reacting. Their expressions were as blank as a sheet of paper and told me nothing. A very handy trick if you don't want your kid to know what you are thinking—I would use it on my kids someday. At that moment, it just raised my stress.

The teacher paused at the end of her recitation and said, "I think your son is bored in class." I looked up, but no one was looking at me. "I think he should be in the English Honors class."

What?

My parents had smiles on their faces. "What do you think, John?"

Are you kidding? I was a teenager in front of a tribunal because of poor grades, and I get something other than yelled at?

"Sure," I mumbled.

And that was that. Little did I know the impact it would have on my life.

Gladys Veidemanis taught English honors. Everyone called her Mrs. V. Transferring into the class in the middle of the year wasn't easy. The class required a lot more reading and writing.

I made it through the year, but I wasn't a fan of the extra work. At the start of the next school year, I tried to go back to regular English class. To my dismay, I realized I had found English Honors less boring (remember, I was a teenager, everything was boring) and transferred back into Mrs. V's class.

In the last two years of high school, Mrs. V assigned lots of books, talking about each one in class. Common themes like "loss of innocence" and "coming of age" dominated the topics, I imagine, because of our age. Those books addressed issues that we, as teenagers, were facing (even if we were clueless about it then).

She made the classes fun, and many of the students connected to her.

I had two close friends in high school and the three of us were in Mrs. V's class. As we got closer to graduation, decisions about college were being made. My two friends chose small liberal arts colleges, and I decided on engineering at a state school.

Engineering may seem like an odd choice for someone as into books as I was. But it wasn't. My dad had a career as an Electrical Engineer and still has a sense of wonder for technology. At a young age, I picked this up from him. I still find the possibilities of technology amazing. So heading to engineering school seemed like the right thing for a kid who, like most, didn't really know what he wanted to be when he grew up.

It felt to me like I became lesser when my engineering choice came out. Because I wasn't going into a program that had lots of English and literature, my friends were more interesting to Mrs. V. Looking back on it from the vantage point of years, that is probably an unfair read of Mrs. V's views, but we can't control what our subconscious picks up, especially as teenagers.

I think I have always had a bit of a chip on my shoulder about this. I enjoyed Mrs. V for her teaching and am thankful for the love of books she contributed to. But to be honest about my motivations, being able to say *See, Mrs. V? I can be an engineer and a writer!* is buried in there somewhere.

My house growing up was full of books. My mom always had at least one book going. My dad took a science fiction class at the local university. I read a couple of his books from the class and fell in love with the genre. The science and wonder caught my attention, and I devoured everything I could get my hands on.

So coming out of high school, I was a big reader, and Mrs. V had taught me books have depth. But, for now, I was a reader, not a writer.

After some floundering around, I got my engineering degree from UW-Madison. Both facts are important in my journey to be a writer.

UW-Madison, at least around 1980, was known as a party school. There was always an element of fun and wackiness. My freshman year, the "Pail & Shovel Party" won the elections for student government. They would get reelected and were the student government most of the time I was there. The name came from a campaign "promise" to redistribute the money from the student government (over $70,000) back to the students by turning it into pennies and giving every student a pail and shovel. They also wanted to fill the football stadium with water to have mock naval battles and bring a life-size replica of the Statue of Liberty to Madison. They actually did the second one.

Pretty creative, eh?

And then there were my engineering classes. While there were some clunkers, most of the classes were interesting.

Sciences are the study of the thing: chemistry is about chemical reactions between molecules, biology is about cells and living things, physics is about fundamental building blocks of everything and the actions that follow.

Engineering is about taking the sciences and making something from them. A chemist will figure out how to create a pill containing a medicine. A chemical engineer will design a manufacturing plant that will make ten thousand of those pills each day. A biologist will figure out how a grasshopper jumps. A mechanical engineer will design an artificial leg that uses some of those properties.

What most people outside of engineering don't realize is that engineering is, at its core, a *creative* job. Sure, engineers have to understand a lot of technical things, but the point of their job is to solve problems and create solutions the world can use. Almost everything you have, touch, eat, or enjoy, has engineering creativity in it.

If you are an engineer, you know a lot about technical theory. You have a set of technical requirements. You design things, often new to the world, relying on your knowledge of good work in the field to, as they say, stand on the shoulders of giants.

How is this different from any artistic endeavor? I imagine that if you looked at your career, there is more creativity in the jobs you held than most people realize.

As was the norm, I took five years to complete the engineering degree. That led to a job at the University of Georgia as an IT system administrator. My degree was in Electrical and Computing Engineering and the Computing part was really fun.

Job led to job. Responsibilities grew. Writing became a larger part of my job. Writing documents, manuals, and application help were part of my daily activities.

In the 1980s, I was at Carleton College when we connected up to some other networks and joined the email infrastructure that was starting on this new thing called 'the Internet'. The era of emails started.

The jobs I had over the years required a lot of emails. The ability to communicate quickly with someone somewhere else was amazing. I enjoyed the writing (and, to be honest, having an audience) and began writing more and longer emails.

This was not always a good thing. In fact, after a few words from a good boss and some comments from others, I realized I needed to cut back on the number of words if I wanted to communicate my message. On more than a few occasions, people didn't read my stuff because it was too long.

So my style became more terse. I tried to have a high signal-to-noise ratio. I aimed to provide slightly less information than people might need or use shorter sentences instead of longer ones. I put summaries in front of my longer emails.

Signal-to-Noise is a concept in engineering that addresses the fact that, in any communication, there is both signal and noise. The signal is the content to be communicated. The noise is anything else the listener or reader experiences.

This term originated in electronic communications but has spread to many other areas. Remember tuning a radio and hearing static? The song you were trying to hear on the station was the signal. The static was the noise. In today's digital world, we may not have actual static, but there is other noise. My emails had too many extra words compared to what I was trying to communicate. To improve the signal-to-noise ratio of my emails, I developed a very terse style.

> *Signal To Noise:*
> *This is a concept in engineering that addresses the fact that, in any communication, there is both signal and noise. The signal is the content to be communicated. The noise is anything else the listener or reader experiences.*

Ten work emails a day, 200 work days a year means 2,000 emails a year. Call it 30 years at that pace for 60,000 work emails. That's a low-end estimate—it was likely much higher, especially adding in personal email. That is a lot of writing.

During my career, I met a few people who had written books. These were the days before ebooks, so they showed off their physical books and I got to hold them in my hand. There was something about seeing a book with the name of someone I knew on the cover. It caught my imagination.

The dream of writing a book had entered my brain. As it was only a dream, I took no action towards it.

That dream would sit there for decades.

In 2018, I got to a point where I wanted to move writing into the Hope stage (more on the dream-hope-plan continuum later). One of my favorite authors was on a writing podcast, *Writing Excuses*. I started listening. It got me thinking so I read and listened to others. Anyone who looks into writing soon comes across the "write every day" advice. I created a document called Practice and started writing most days. At first a couple of paragraphs, then gradually getting longer.

Here is my first entry, unedited.

7/22/2018

The room was quiet, not silent. The pre-teen's pencil scritched across the paper as she drew. The occasional bird song came in through the open windows. The morning sun was on the other side of the house. While there wasn't any sun streaming in the windows, it was lighting up the trees out the large picture windows on the two outside walls. The younger granddaughter sat next to her sister staring silently out the window. The two of them had woken up fifteen minutes earlier and wandered in from the living room where they had spent the night. Gave grandma and grandpa a hug good morning and settled into the sofa. The older one was about 5 minutes ahead of her sister in the waking up and had started drawing. The two cups of coffee steamed up gently.

It felt weird just writing something that wasn't for work or an email to family. It was just for me. I didn't even show it to my wife.

I kept at it, writing single paragraphs about this and that. Memories from high school, snippets from my day, a scene from my drive home.

Eventually, I started making stuff up. Sometimes trying to imagine a character and writing a few paragraphs about them doing something. Sometimes describing someone I knew doing something I was aware of, but not something that had happened.

Another thing they say is to "write what you know." I knew this would eventually be nonsense—how else can anyone write science fiction or fantasy or anything not rooted in cold reality—but for now, it was helpful. The people, places, and things I knew about were the things I wrote about.

Music was another thing that I knew about. Not anything about playing, I was strictly a listener. The piano lessons in fourth grade didn't take, but music was always playing in the house. A few of my practice entries were about playing music or being a musician.

About five months after I started, I wrote my first short story. I had discovered a live music video on YouTube called "Learn To Fly - Foo Fighters Rockin'1000 Official Video" on the Rockin' 1000 channel. Guitarists, bassists, drummers, and singers—one thousand musicians in total—in one place and one time to play one song they all loved. I still get goosebumps every time I watch the joy and sheer scale of the video.

I knew there were at least a thousand actual stories, one per person, about that day and wondered if I could write a fictional one. I picked a face from the video and made up a story about how they got to the scene. The result was "Cesana", which, while clearly written by a rookie writer, felt like an accomplishment.

Around this time, a friend of mine sent out an email about a new writing group. Her sister-in-law (a published author) was moving to town and wanted to start up a writing group like she used to be in.

I had no idea what a writing group did. But I knew I needed to learn to share my work, and I wanted feedback from others. So I joined.

We called ourselves Ex-Libris Writers II (ELWII) for reasons only important to ourselves. At each session, each of us read something and the group provided feedback. Our personalities led us to mainly pointing out what we liked and how to strengthen the piece. We seemed (and still seem) far from the "tough critic" model of writers' groups.

My stories got longer and characters even started showing up multiple times. A character named Matilda showed up in a few short stories. I got this character from a few people I know that are excellent at mechanical kinds of things. Throw something new—and broken—at them and they can figure out how it works and how to fix it. Matilda's stories came out of wondering what would happen if these people got their hands on "alien tech" (remember, I have a science fiction interest).

The folks at ELWII liked Matilda and a few of my other stories, and that gave me confidence. I highly recommend getting into a supportive writer's group that helps you get better. New writers need to be told what they are doing right more than they need to be corrected.

At some point, the idea for an IT leadership book came to me. I had a 30+ year career in IT, most of it in leadership, and had lots of opinions about how to run an IT organization. What if I wrote a book for IT leaders to share some of that knowledge?

So I did. Kennd Publishing published *The I.T. Leaders' Handbook* worldwide in March 2020.

Wow, that was a learning experience.

I get ahead of myself. Back in 2019, I was still struggling with this retirement idea. And I had started writing. However, I hadn't connected them yet. I wanted to be a writer. I needed to have something to retire TO before I could retire. Two independent ideas.

I had heard stories about people retiring and being bored out of their minds. I had known a few of those people. Sometimes, it had a negative impact on their health.

I figured I would do some volunteering. Both my mom and dad do that and it seems like a default activity for retirement, but that didn't really hold much excitement for me. At least not at that point in my life.

When I thought about retirement, it felt like it would be a *I'm done, now what?* kind of thing. I didn't want to be done.

One day, those two things, retiring and writing, ran into each other in my brain. It wasn't a momentous occasion where the stars aligned, music swelled in the background, and the wisdom of the gods filled my soul. It was probably sitting in our sunroom watching a TV show that wasn't holding my interest.

I decided in that moment that, when I retired in a few years, I would retire to become a writer.

This is my story. It won't be yours, but maybe you will find some inspiration or ideas that help you create your own story.

Chapter 2: Benefits of Being Retirement Age

Aging these decades
Experience, Wisdom, Life
Gives us a head start

We are older than we used to be. No way to put that differently. We can't change our age no matter how much we lie about it. But old does not mean infirm or incapable. Old also means wise, knowledgeable, and compassionate. We, and society, spend too little time on understanding the benefits of getting old.

I believe that getting older provides us three things that we didn't have when we were younger:

- Experiences.

- Perspective.

- Self-Awareness.

All three are important to our writing. I'll talk about them in more detail in this chapter.

One note before we get into these benefits. These are benefits for you *compared to your younger self*. How it compares to others is not relevant. If you think that your experiences or perspectives or self-awareness are better or worse than others', you are missing the point. Learn from others? Definitely. Be inspired by others? Absolutely. But *comparisonitis* is a major demotivator. Why do that to yourself?

You should only ever compare yourself to yourself.

Getting older gives you more experiences than when you were younger. It doesn't give you experiences other people have.

You have a deeper perspective on life. You don't have the same perspective as anyone else. It gives you more self-awareness than you had when you were younger. It may or may not give you more self-awareness than others.

If you are worried about being "behind" by starting in retirement, don't be.

Laura Ingalls Wilder (in her sixties), Raymond Chandler (forties), Mary Wesley (technically fifties, but not really until her seventies) all started doing something new later in life. Richard Adams didn't write his first novel, *Watership Down*, until his fifties.

And not just writers. Grandma Moses started painting in her seventies. Mary Delany invented her "paper mosaics" in her seventies—you can see them in the British Museum. Harland Sanders didn't start making chicken until his forties, and started Kentucky Fried Chicken in his sixties. Julia Child didn't start cooking until her forties.

Those are just the people that became popular. The number of people who picked up something new in their retirement and loved it but didn't become famous is huge. You probably know a few of them.

If you had children, you know about longer time frames. The time from diapers to moving out went by way too fast, but was only a couple of decades. According to the United States Centers for Disease Control (CDC) in 2016, the life expectancy of a 65-year-old averages almost fifteen years and continues to increase (CDC, Health, United States, 2019 - Data Finder, retrieved November 12, 2021). We may have almost as long to write as it took to raise our kids. Think of what you were like when your kids were born and what you were like when they were teenagers. Those fifteen years were a time where we grew as well as our kids.

You've got decades behind you. You may have decades ahead of you.

Let's look at why you are in a good place to become a writer.

More Experiences

One advantage of getting older is that we are not dead yet. Not being dead means we continue to accumulate experiences. The quantity and variety of these experiences become a resource for our creativity. We have more experiences, and therefore more creative resources, than we did yesterday, last year, or twenty years ago.

While our subconscious is a mysterious thing that no one really understands, I believe it acts, in part, as a compost pile for our experiences.

Compost piles are amazing things that convert old stuff into new stuff. The compost pile most of us are familiar with takes all sorts of kitchen scraps or yard waste and creates very fertile dirt that we can use to grow beautiful and tasty things.

Our subconscious does the same thing with our experiences.

Everything we experience goes into our subconscious, our internal compost pile. We don't know how; we don't know when, but at some point, interesting things grow. I'll cover that more in the chapter on "Where Do Ideas Come From?".

Our life experiences include everything. Family, work, friends, community. It includes both good and bad experiences. It includes the things we did and didn't do. It includes the thoughts and emotions about both.

Each of us is a unique combination of experiences. Some of our experiences have happened to others. I'm certainly not the only left-handed, classic rock music fan who worked in IT. Some experiences are unique to us and have never happened to another human in history. No one else in history has ever had the experience of being me in my particular family.

We have spent a lifetime of working. Different jobs had different tasks we had to do with different people. We've had multiple supervisors and probably different companies.

We have seen drama, comedy, and tragedy in our jobs. We have seen kindness, compassion, rudeness, and meanness in our coworkers. All of this can feed our storytelling.

We have had lucky breaks, and we have had bad luck. We have had successes, and we have had failures. The characters in our stories will have them as well.

Think of the people that have influenced you over the years. The boss that took care of you during a rough time. The coworker that always took the time to teach you. The new employee that appreciated your help.

In our family life, we have experienced generations. The people that raised us. Our extended family. As we got older, the younger generation came along and we were in the middle with both older and younger relatives. Now that we are retirement age, the younger generation is larger and the older generation takes more of our concern.

Each of our families is unique. Your family experiences differ from mine, indeed, they differ from everyone else on the planet. That difference, that uniqueness, which you have lived for decades, gives you a set of experiences that no one else can bring to their writing.

You tried new things. Sometimes you succeeded. Sometimes you failed. Sometimes you weren't sure either way. You may have not tried something new and always regretted it. You may have chosen not to try something, and it was the perfect decision.

You fell in love. You fell out of love. You got confused about love.

You have experienced the sense of loss that only comes after years of connection.

You have experienced the sense of connection that only comes after loss.

You have experienced wonderful people. You have experienced inspirational people. You have experienced positive people.

You have experienced negative people. You have experienced deeply wounded people who lash out at others in their pain. You have experienced evil.

> *The decades you have been living, regardless of what you might think about them, were spent accumulating experiences that your younger self never dreamed of. These experiences will have a profound impact on your writing.*

The decades you have been living, regardless of what you might think about them, were spent accumulating experiences that your younger self never dreamed of. These experiences will have a profound impact on your writing.

But those aren't the only experiences we can draw on.

When we think about life experiences, we don't always include the media we consume. However, as writers, every show, book, song, and movie we experience goes into that compost pile. We liked some of them. We didn't like others.

Whether we will write fiction or non-fiction, our compost pile is much deeper than it was when we were thirty years old. The experience of our years gives us more to draw on for ideas and inspiration.

Better Perspective

Another benefit of getting old is the sense of perspective you develop. There is a quote I (mostly) remember from many years ago. I think it was Andy Rooney who said it, but I can't find evidence of it, so I can't be sure. It goes something like this.

> *It is with great satisfaction that I look back and realize how much wiser, how much smarter I am than five years ago. That satisfaction is tempered by the fact that I will most assuredly be saying the same thing five years from now.*

Years provide perspective. We have seen the results of decisions, choices, behaviors. We have learned what is important and what doesn't really matter in the long run.

Remember how big a deal high school graduation was at the time? How do you think about it now? Remember the excitement of your first job? Where does that fit in the milestones of your life? Remember your first crush? Remember your first favorite musician?

Don't get me wrong—all these events were significant and influential. I'm not diminishing any of them. I am saying that, in a longer lifetime, we gain a useful perspective about it all.

That job you didn't get? Massively disappointing at the time, but maybe left you available for a better job.

The divorce that was soul-crushing at the time? Maybe it left you in a position to make the next relationship work better. Or it taught you a bit more about how the world worked.

Our age helps us understand the long-term view. We know the years will always go by and events will always look different down the road. When we were younger, we cared more about the short term. What was happening this weekend was more important than what we were doing next month. Why did it matter if we cleaned our room or not? As we got older, we were living with more of our decisions and directly experienced how short-term thinking could bite us.

We know that everything that is built needs maintenance, as nothing lasts forever. We learned what happened if we didn't take care of our car, house, or relationships. We know that if we don't take care of things, they won't last.

We all put something off, only to regret not taking care of it sooner.

We learned that if we worked at something, we could figure it out or accomplish something that, in our twenties, we would not have thought possible.

We have seen many successes and failures and have developed a gut sense about whether a new change will work. We have a hard time explaining this gut feeling because it isn't based on facts; it is based on perspective.

We know there is a gap between what we think we should do and what we will actually do. We know what we can change about ourselves and what we can't.

This perspective of the years results from living as long as we have. We have a better perspective on life now than we did when we were younger. Perspective is necessary for telling stories. Each of our characters has a unique perspective of the situations we throw them into. Our non-fiction is better than we would have written thirty years ago because of that perspective of what matters.

The perspective gained from living until retirement age makes us better writers.

Deeper Self-Awareness

The third benefit of being retirement age is our sense of self-awareness. Simply put, we know ourselves much better than we did when we were younger. This self-awareness makes us a little more surefooted as we head out on this writing journey.

The years have taught us our strengths and weaknesses. They have taught us what we like and don't like. We can use this knowledge to navigate our unique path.

If we know we don't get far without a plan and someone holding us to it, then we create that plan and find that person. If we know we rebel against grandiose plans, then we set out in a direction and feel our way along the journey.

We have also learned that we frequently get in our own way. I'll talk more about this in "Chapter 3: Your Opponent". For now, realize that some of the negative assessments in your self-awareness may not be true.

What else do we know about ourselves?

We have put things off and regretted it. We jumped into things too quickly. We have learned what we enjoy and what we don't. What we enjoy changed over time.

We learn how we learn. We know what kinds of things we can learn easily and what takes more work. We have learned a tremendous amount in our lifetime. We know how to do it and we know what works best. Since we will have to learn in order to be a writer, we can use this knowledge to our advantage.

We changed jobs and needed to learn a new skill set. We changed careers and had to learn how to do something completely different. Whether or not we enjoyed our careers, we learned what kinds of things we liked to work on. Not every job is perfect, and every job has something to like about it. In our twenties and thirties, we had a limited sense of what we liked to do. Over time, as our experiences expanded, we did things we like, and we did things we didn't like. Here we are nearing retirement and we have a better sense of what we like and don't like.

A lifetime of working has shown us hard work. We did it ourself. We watched others do it. We saw that hard work, whether at work or in our personal lives, got us more than not. We have the experience of finishing projects we started. When we put the time in, we accomplished more.

Maybe it was physically hard work. Maybe it was mental or emotional hard work. Either way, as someone approaching retirement, we have simply had more opportunities to learn that working hard gets us more. Of course, that isn't always the case, but when supervisors, companies, governments, or family were not involved, we would accomplish more with hard work than without it.

Our self-awareness tells us what parts of the day are better than others for different tasks. At this point in our lives, we know if we do better in the early morning or the late evening. We know what bad habits get in our way, and we know which bad habits we might be able to change.

A lifetime has taught us that our view of ourselves doesn't always match that of others. They may see more good things about ourselves than we do. We chalk it up to the imposter syndrome (also covered in the "Chapter 3: Your Opponent"), but maybe, just maybe, we can learn about ourselves from others.

While self-awareness can be a double-edge sword, I think it is overall a good thing. If we are serious about becoming a writer, we can leverage what we know about ourselves to make better progress on our journey.

Chapter 3: Your Opponent

*Creativity
The Opponent will do all
It can to stop it*

The Force Against You

So we have talked about the benefits of being older when we start our writing journey. Now I would like to talk about the strongest force against you. I call it the *Opponent*.

This Opponent will do anything it can to ensure our failure. The Opponent lives for the short-term and doesn't like any hard work, especially towards long-term plans. The Opponent keeps us from starting things. It keeps us from finishing things. It empties the optimism from our soul as fast as a football team empties a pizza buffet.

And most of all? Our Opponent doesn't like anything creative. It hates creativity with the anger of a small child refusing to go to bed, throwing temper tantrums into our brain to derail us.

As we have gotten better with age, so has our Opponent. It has years of figuring out how to prevent us from being creative. It knows what works and what doesn't.

This Opponent is not something that we can stop. We can't destroy it. At best, we can keep it at bay through attitude, discipline and habit. In order to become a writer, we must fight our Opponent constantly.

Your Opponent may be telling you, right at this moment, to put down this book because this is all a bunch of nonsense and who are you to think you could be a writer, anyway?

This Opponent is, of course, us. It lives inside our head. It is the voice inside us pointing out shiny objects and criticizing our work before, during, and after we have done it. It knows exactly what to say to stop us from moving forward. The Opponent will cause us to procrastinate and will cripple us with self-doubt. This double-whammy will provide a constant headwind against our writing.

In his masterful book, *The War of Art*, Stephen Pressfield (see "Resources") describes *Resistance*. He says, "Resistance is not a peripheral opponent. Resistance arises from within. It is self-generated and self-perpetuated. Resistance is the enemy within."

Our Opponent fights us in two ways.

Distraction

Our Opponent distracts us with shiny objects. It points out other things we want to be doing. It points out stupid stuff we did as a teenager. It reminds us that Aunt Maria isn't doing well and why haven't we called her? Social media is a wonderland in the Opponent's hands, always pulling us in to doomscroll or watch cat videos. When we think about writing, the Opponent will remind us of every one of the other things we should be doing.

Tim Urban (see "Resources"), creator at WaitButWhy.com, gave a legendary, and hilarious, TED Talk called Inside the Mind of a Master Procrastinator (~14 minutes) where he introduces us to the Instant Gratification Monkey. The Instant Gratification Monkey is a very persuasive creature that lives inside our heads. Whenever the rational part of your brain wants to steer the ship, the Monkey grabs the wheel and sends you in a non-productive direction.

In fact, while looking up the specific URL to include in this book, my Instant Gratification Monkey took me down the rabbit hole of the WaitButWhy website for twenty minutes before I remembered that this was my writing time.

The Opponent never misses an opportunity to distract us from our goal.

Self-Doubt

The Opponent also belittles us and tells us to give up this writing thing because we are clearly the worst writer ever. Or would be the worst if we actually tried.

This is our Opponent making us afraid. In her book *Big Magic*, Elizabeth Gilbert, author of *Eat, Pray, Love* and other delightful books, talks about fear this way. "Your fear will always be triggered by your creativity, because creativity asks you to enter into the realms of uncertain outcome, and fear hates uncertain outcome."

Another way our Opponent creates self-doubt is by pointing out the success of others. We have experienced good art, but our first attempts won't match up. We read famous authors or best-sellers and our Opponent just uses it as ammunition for future attacks.

The Opponent compares our efforts, our first drafts, our ideas to finished products that are on the market. This is comparing apples to oranges. The Opponent compares our first drafts to the finished books we have read. Those books were written by people that likely wrote a rough first draft and then cleaned it up, usually with help from one or more editors. That's like comparing some initial sketches of a new car design to the finished car coming off the production line. Or comparing your first pencil sketch to a finished painting in a museum. Or comparing the draft of your first short story to the final draft of an award-winning short story. It makes no sense when we think about it, but the Opponent is not logical.

> *The Opponent compares our efforts, our first drafts, our ideas to finished products that are on the market. This is comparing apples to oranges.*

The Opponent will weaponize our internal editor against us. Experienced writers tell us to turn off our inner editor when writing the first draft. The Opponent thinks that is a load of rubbish and will try to turn on the editor part of our brain. While learning to write better first drafts is a good learning goal, the Opponent doesn't care about that, it just wants us to trip over every comma, misspelling, and passive voice that might be there—anything to derail the writing process.

The Relationship Between Us and the Opponent

The Opponent's tools, distraction and self-doubt, are insidious, powerful, and ever present. My Opponent will get in my way at any opportunity. "I'm no good at this." "This story sucks." "No one will buy this." "Ooh, look, Twitter!" "That's a stupid opening sentence." "This is a great story! You will never write anything this good, so why try?" "I'll just watch one more episode." "Look, just watch this short video about animated hedgehogs, it will just take a minute."

You may have heard of the *Imposter Syndrome*, the fear that you really are incompetent regardless of your successes, and it is only a matter of time before everyone else realizes it, too. This is the Opponent whispering in your ear.

Your Opponent will differ from mine. It will use your personality against you. To survive, we must understand what our particular Opponent is like. We must understand how our particular Opponent fights against us.

One advantage of us being retirement age is that we have lots of experience fighting with the Opponent. We won some; we lost some. We may not have recognized the Opponent for what it was, but, looking back, we recognize its handiwork. The types of tasks you had a hard time completing. The dreams you gave up on. The negative daydreaming when trying to work. The new things you tried, but gave up on quickly.

The downside of us being retirement age is that the Opponent is older also and has more experience stopping our creativity. Remember back to that job you decided not to apply for? Or that adventure you didn't go on? The Opponent remembers the techniques that successfully derailed us and uses them again and again.

Often, the Opponent will shove irrelevant questions into our brain. Why try to learn anything new? Who would want to read what I write? What do I have to offer the world?

A lot, actually. Each of us is a unique person offering the world a unique viewpoint. Our lifetime of personal experiences has never been duplicated in all of human history. Each of us has something unique to offer the world. We can turn this uniqueness, even if we don't understand it, into a shield to fend off the Opponent's attacks.

As an adult, we are doing so many things that would have mystified and terrified us when we were kids. Getting a job, paying taxes, being in a relationship, maybe having kids, fixing a car. We have learned an amazing amount, and became good at many things, to become a functioning adult. We have already figured out how to learn, practice, and get better.

As we look at retirement, we can pull on what we know about habits and techniques that work for us. We have experience learning, so we may have an idea about how we learn. We have past successes we can draw on. Remember these.

We must be compassionate with ourselves when we lose battles with the Opponent. Because we will. No one wins all the battles. When we lose a battle, say watching a movie instead of writing, the Opponent will then use *that* 'failure' to tell us we must not really want to be a writer after all, so just give up. Did I mention our Opponent is a right bastard?

Don't focus on the losses, focus on the wins. If you can win one minor battle today, you have a better chance of winning another one tomorrow. And two more next week.

All this will help us on our journey to become the writer we want to be. Here are a few other things that can help.

- We are already a creative person. Daved G. Driscoll (see "Resources"), a creativity expert that has taught youth and adults for years, puts forth that creativity is hard-wired into each person. Creativity is an innate human attribute. In my opinion, we often can't see our creativity because the Opponent is hiding it from us. Like Disneyland hiding all the trash collection, our Opponent will make us believe our creativity doesn't exist. But it does. Creativity is already within us.

- Pull positive feedback from everywhere possible. This internal battle against the Opponent is the hardest one we will ever face. We don't need to face it all by ourselves. Humans are, at our core, social creatures, and feedback from other people matters. Find people that help and eliminate those that are on the Opponent's side. If you have the misfortune of having a family member or friend that, no matter how well meaning, is saying the same things the Opponent is, avoid those conversations. The battle with our Opponent is hard enough as it is.

- Look for constructive criticism. While this may seem in conflict with looking for positive feedback, it isn't. You will not get better without constructive feedback. This can come from a writing group, an editor, or a peer. Remember that our Opponent will prevent us from dispassionately evaluating our work. Find people you trust to provide positive feedback and constructive feedback.

- Look for examples. The more you read, the more you will build an idea of what is good writing. This idea will be a weird combination of punctuation and grammar rules and deeply personal opinions like topics, stories, endings, etc. This idea of good writing will be unique to you. You will know what you like and this should guide your writing. The Opponent will try to devalue what you like. For years I put down what I liked, saying "I like trashy science fiction." Then someone asked me to define trashy, and I realized that was just a word I used as a putdown just in case I was talking to a person who didn't like science fiction. It was the Opponent speaking, demeaning what I liked.

- We will never attain perfection, so don't try to make your writing perfect. Remember that perfect is the enemy of good. You will get to a point where you need to send your work out into the world and it won't be perfect. Too bad, send it anyway. Contests are great for this because they have a deadline that forces us to send it whether or not we think it is ready. But if we do the work, we will get better. Small steps over time results in enormous improvements. If the Opponent can't stop you from writing, it will try to get you to make the writing perfect so you never finish.

To recap, the Opponent is inside each of us. Even all those famous authors we look up to. The Opponent will try to distract us and make us doubt our ability. We can fight back with understanding, acceptance, habits, and compassion. We need to focus on our wins, not our losses.

What I Am Doing

The Opponent doesn't just fight against our writing. We have been fighting our Opponent in all aspects of life. It kept us from applying for that job outside our field. It kept us from speaking up against the crowd. It kept us from learning something new. It kept us from getting that report done on time.

Personally, my Opponent knows I can be easily distracted by technology and process. Trying out a new application because it might be useful someday is not a bad thing. Doing it when I have performance reviews to write is a bad thing. If I needed to clean up the laundry room or garage, I would spend more time figuring out how I was going to clean it than actually cleaning it.

I would read the news when I needed to get work done. I would watch one more episode instead of cleaning up after dinner. I would head over to talk to another manager rather than work on the quarterly department report.

Self-doubt has also been a challenge in my career. Being in a leadership position requires that I make decisions that impact people's lives and the success of the business. There is never enough information to make decisions, which creates a lot of room for doubt and second-guessing. There have been opportunities I didn't reach out for because I doubted my abilities.

Here is something that happened repeatedly over my career. In situations where I had to send an email that not all the recipients would be happy about, I would have the hardest time hitting the Send button. I would reread the email far too many times, looking for typos, awkward sentences, anything to improve. All I was really doing was stalling.

Looking back, I realize my Opponent has existed my entire life. And now, in retirement, I was about to enter a creative endeavor which would enrage my Opponent and take its fight to a whole new level. I had to do something.

Understanding that my Opponent existed was the first step. This helped me realize I could do something about it. I could fight back. And it is a fight. Those that tell you it is only about will and determination are vastly oversimplifying the problem. I needed to have a plan.

And once you realize the Opponent will get in the way of planning how to beat the Opponent, you are on your way to truly understanding how devious the Opponent is.

How I think about my Opponent

My Opponent lives in a drab little room that is always messy and very dark. No windows. He eats mac & cheese three meals a day and hates it. He has no music, TV, or books. My Opponent's lack of discipline and self-doubt makes him very cranky, and he takes it out on me whenever he sees me being, or about to be, productive.

My Opponent seems to get a particular kick out of imagining future situations where things don't turn out well. Imagining conversations of others where they are bad-mouthing my work. Imagining my books failing to sell.

Words of defiance from Elizabeth Gilbert's Big Magic have helped me.

> *"What if people absolutely hate what you've created? What if people attack you with savage vitriol, and insult your intelligence, and malign your motive, and drag your good name through the mud? Just smile sweetly and suggest—as politely as you possibly can—that they go make their own fucking art. Then stubbornly continue making yours.*
> *—Elizabeth Gilbert"*

The Opponent wants me to imagine all the horrible things people might say. It can be very creative. There are many people in the world and most won't like my writing. I can accept that as true but come to a different conclusion. My Opponent will use it as a reason to quit. I just see it as a truth and focus on the ones that *will* like my writing.

Most people, in reality, won't even read my writing because they won't be aware of it. Obscurity is a bigger threat to me than rejection. I can do something about obscurity (Publish more books! Tell people about them!), but I can't do anything about rejection.

I know I still have work to do in this fight. With Gilbert's words, I know in my head that I shouldn't care what others think, but I'm pretty sure my heart is still early in that understanding. Something to keep working on.

Here's another one from my Opponent's greatest hits. It has maintained a catalog of recordings from events in my life where I made a mistake, embarrassed myself, or did something I regret. This catalog has both significant and trivial events and goes back to early school days. At the most inopportune times, my Opponent will press play on one of these memory recordings. The memory will always play at full volume in my head.

Because the Opponent seems to have only high-fidelity recordings, all the emotions from the original situation come along for the ride. I have a physical reaction when these playbacks occur. This will derail me from whatever I was working on.

I haven't mastered my Opponent. It still kicks my butt too frequently. But I know it is there and I know I need to fight or my plan for writing will die.

How I fight the Opponent

I am fighting my Opponent with two approaches: flexibility and habits. These two might seem opposites of each other. And to be honest, they do conflict. However, they each have their place. Remember, this is what I am trying to do and may not work for you. Heck, it might not even work for me, but I'm fighting.

First, I use flexibility to increase the times and places that I can write. While having a specific writing place is important, I want to make sure I can write anywhere. For example, my wife and I enjoy camping. Heading into retirement, we hope to do a lot more. If I can't write at a campsite because it isn't my dedicated writing place, I will have a conflict between wanting to camp and wanting to write.

Second, I selected a writing tool (Dabble) that stores my writing in the cloud and works on any device. This allows me to use my phone, my laptop, someone else's laptop, or whatever device is nearby. I have access to all my writing projects and can write anytime, anywhere. The tool also works offline, so I don't need a network connection to write.

Third, I try to write in lots of situations. Different times of the day. Different places. Waiting at the doctor's office. Mornings by the campfire. Standing in a line with my phone. Not all of them work very well, but capturing even a few words or an idea moves me forward.

Habits have made a big difference for me. Over the past two years, the one that has made the most difference is writing first thing in the morning. And by "first thing", I mean get out of bed, throw on sweats, pour a cup of coffee (coffee maker timers are awesome!) and sit down and write. No phone, no conversation, no internet.

This gets me a good hour of writing before the rest of the day starts. Recently, I started planning in the evening for the next morning's writing. I open my writing tool, make sure I know what portion of the book I will work on, and think about what I will write in the morning. I figure that this helps my subconscious get a head start. Not sure if this works or not, but it is something to try.

Another habit I am trying is affirmations. Affirmations are short sentences you repeat to yourself many times over the course of the day. They are usually future state. I first heard the term listening to an interview with Scott Adams, creator of the *Dilbert* comic strip. I remembered I had used the same technique at the advice of my therapist when I was going through my divorce.

One thing that surprised me was how angry the Opponent got at the idea of affirmations. Thinking about using affirmations myself would bring a wave a "that's stupid! It will never work!" The Opponent's response was far stronger than almost anything else it would fight against.

Hmm... interesting.

Is it possible that my Opponent knew more than I did about the effectiveness of affirmations? No idea. But I figured if doing affirmations made the Opponent angry, that must mean they are a good thing to try. The Opponent hates all the other good stuff I am trying to do, so maybe affirmations would work.

At the beginning, I simply used "I am a writer." Writers write, so if I wrote, I am a writer. That is different from being an author, a blogger, or a journalist. It only refers to putting words together into larger groups of words. Over time, I have changed it to "I will be a published author" and then to "I will be a multi-series profitable author."

When one of my ELWII writers' group pointed out that affirmations have scientific proof that they work for both physical and mental issues, well, that was a bonus. Patients using affirmations reported better recovery than those that didn't.

There were a few times when a particular battle with the Opponent was at a tipping point and I remembered the affirmation.

This helped move things back my way. If it helps me win a few battles, I'll keep trying it.

Taking small steps and small risks can help fight against the Opponent. When you are walking into a strong headwind, small steps help. Small risks help you understand that writing won't kill you. Small steps and small risks lead to small wins. Small wins, over time, turn into bigger wins. I'll go into that in a little more detail in the next section.

Here are some of the small steps I took.

- Every day, sitting down and just writing whatever was in my head without judgement. No one sees my practice document.
- Writing dialogue for the first time. Writing lots of little bits of dialogue. Again without judgement.
- Finding podcasts to listen to on my commute and trying some of the writing exercises they suggested.
- Writing gradually longer pieces. First a couple of sentences, then a paragraph, then a page, then a chapter, then a book. That took time, of course, but each small step added up.

Some of the small risks I took.

- Sharing my writing with Joyce.
- Sharing my writing with family.
- Sharing my writing with the Ex Libris II writing group.
- Posting my writing on my website.
- Entering my first contest.

The small steps and small risks were hard at the time. It took me over an hour to hit send on the email entering that first contest. But they were low-risk enough that the Opponent didn't get too cranky. Remember that the Opponent can't see long term, it only thinks short term. So small steps might not be threatening. My Opponent would just sit there in the dark with its bowl of mac & cheese, shaking its head at my apparent stupidity, not realizing that I was making progress with these small steps and small risks.

> Remember that the Opponent can't see long term, it only thinks short term.

The positivity of the ELWII writing group helped as well. We focused on what we liked about each piece and a few suggested improvements. Getting positive feedback helped my confidence a little each time. The Opponent succeeds by destroying our confidence, so we give up. This external encouragement is critical to a new writer. I believe that positive feedback creates space in our confidence for receiving improvement suggestions.

The Opponent will always push back on your writing, just like it did throughout your entire life and career up to now. Recognize that it has the attention span of a squirrel and the psyche of a small, scared child. Thinking of the Opponent as a separate entity from yourself can help you fight it when it tries to derail your writing.

The Opponent will be your biggest challenge. If you take away one thing from this book, it is this: the Opponent is actively working against you and the sooner you realize this, and start fighting back, the better off you will be in all aspects of life.

Small Steps

There is an old joke: How do you eat an elephant? One bite at a time. The Chinese proverb, "a journey of a thousand miles begins with a single step", puts forth the same idea with more elegance.

Embrace this concept.

Thinking about being a writer can be overwhelming. If you scan through this or other "how to be an author" books, there is a lot to learn. We have to learn craft, we have to learn the tools, and we have to learn the business if we want others to see our work. Each of these topics is very large and each worthy of a lifetime of study.

But we don't want to spend a lifetime learning to be an author. We want to write. How do you balance learning with doing? To me, the answer is simple.

Take small steps.

Anything significant we do is made up of small steps. Maybe we aren't conscious of them. We don't think of raising children or working a career as a set of small steps, but they were.

In your career, you have seen this a thousand times. The end of the day closing process at a restaurant, any manufacturing process, an engineer's design project, a plumber fixing a leaky sink, teaching a class. These jobs are all series of small steps.

Let's talk about this plumber a little more. Plumbers go through an apprentice program to learn their skills. Unlike going to college, plumbers produce work early in their learning process. They learn a bit, use it to do work, then learn a little more.

This is how I think about writing. I am in an apprenticeship. I will learn and produce work at the same time. This is possible only if you think about the learning, and doing, in terms of small steps.

> Let's talk about this plumber a little more. Plumbers go through an apprentice program to learn their skills. Unlike going to college, plumbers produce work early in their learning process. They learn a bit, use it to do work, then learn a little more.

You don't sit down to write a book in one sitting. You don't even write the first draft in one sitting. You write a set of words and come back tomorrow to do it again.

It is easier to think about larger projects in terms of small steps. It's overwhelming to think about writing, formatting, and publishing a book. But breaking it down into small steps makes it doable.

Small steps allow us to make progress learning and writing each week. Small steps also allow us to adjust to changing situations easier than large steps.

Consider this. You are at home. The lights are all out; it is the dead of night, and the nightlights are on. Given that we are near retirement age, we are all getting up at least once during the night to go to the bathroom. If you aren't there yet, count your blessings. Anyway, we get up and walk to the bathroom as we have done many times before.

But we still take smaller steps than we would if it was in the middle of a bright day.

Why? Because, when we are unsure of the path and can't see clearly, we take smaller steps to keep our footing and avoid stubbing our toes.

And that is for going from the bed to the bathroom, something we have done many (many! sigh) times. Becoming a writer is something that we have done exactly zero times before. We don't know the path because we haven't walked it before.

Not only haven't we walked this path before, we don't even know where it is. We can read stories of the paths of others, but ours will be unique. We must discover it ourselves.

Take small steps.

When wondering what to do, take a small step in the direction you want to go. Practicing is taking small steps. Listening to podcasts or reading books on writing is taking small steps. Showing your work to one person is a small step. Learning a new software is a small step.

Take small steps. And do it again tomorrow. Keep doing this and you will travel a thousand miles.

Small Risks

Starting any large endeavor carries risks. Starting an artistic endeavor, like retiring to become a writer, carries more risks.

But these risks won't kill us. These risks are failure, embarrassment, not meeting our own expectations, and a host of others. The biggest risk is that we will give up. While not fatal to our physical body, it can be devastating to go from dream to hope to plan to giving up.

This is the Big Quit. Quitting on the dream of being a writer, an author, a creative person. There is an old adage that says "what doesn't kill us makes us stronger". Angela Duckworth (see "Resources"), author of the excellent book *Grit*, makes an important modification to this. She says "What doesn't kill us makes us stronger, unless it makes us quit."

This book is about becoming a writer after we retire. The fact you are reading this shows this is something you are thinking about. Presuming you are serious about becoming a writer, the Big Quit is your biggest risk.

All the other things about writing that scare you only matter if it keeps you from moving forward. If you have the courage to keep moving forward in the face of the fear, you can avoid the Big Quit. Applying the concept we just learned about small steps, we can see that there is a way we can build up the courage we need.

Take small risks.

Show your work to one new person. Try a different opening sentence. Try a different style of dialogue. Enter a writing contest.

Taking small risks has two primary benefits. The first is similar to the Take Small Steps message of the last section. By taking small risks, we make small progress. By doing it again tomorrow and the day after and next week, we expand what we are capable of. Because risks, like steps, are progress toward our goal. Sometimes your small step will be taking a small risk.

The second benefit is that taking small risks is like exercise. The more we do, the more we are able to do. Taking a small risk, say showing our writing to one person, makes it easier to take a slightly larger risk, say joining a writing group.

Like steps are cumulative, risks help build the courage and experience to take larger risks. Succeeding at small risks teaches us that this writing thing won't kill us. It teaches us we can do more.

I believe we are capable of more than we think we are. It isn't the outside world that is keeping us from being a writer, but it is our Opponent that causes most of the problems.

Sometimes, a small risk will fail. That's why it's called a risk, not a step. Small failures are easier to deal with than large ones. If the first time we show our work to an outside person is after we have finished an 80,000 word book, we are taking a bigger risk than if our first sharing is of a short story.

Consider chopping wood. If we start small and then chop a little more each day, we build up calluses on our hands. If, the first time we chop, we chop for eight hours, our hands will be a bloody mess.

Taking small risks builds calluses on our determination. These calluses can protect us from future failure. Each day of chopping makes it possible to chop for longer tomorrow. Each day of taking small risks makes it possible to take bigger risks tomorrow.

Writing in general, and becoming an author specifically, is a risky proposition. But the risks won't kill us. Being thoughtful about getting better at dealing with the risk pays off in the long run.

Take small risks.

Chapter 4: The Journey

Dreams are shiny things
Hopes are the first feeble step
Plans move us forward

Dreams, Hopes, Plans

By deciding to become a writer, we are embarking on a journey different from our career. Sure, when we first left school, we may have known what we wanted to do, but most of us have a career that wasn't all planned out. But here we are, deciding to be a writer when we retire.

We chose to finish our career before we jumped into writing. Maybe you have long dreamed of being a writer. Maybe, like me, it was a recent dream. Each writer comes to this journey differently.

Dreams. Hopes. Plans. That's the progression. If something is a Dream, you only think about it. Or think about having done it. A Dream is a wish. It floats around in your head, maybe coming out to play when in conversation with others. We daydream about them. We imagine ourselves doing whatever we are dreaming about and it is wonderful.

Sometimes we take a step or two in the dream's direction. This is the Hope stage. We read about it. We spend a little money. We spend a little time. We might even have some steps we imagine we would take. But we are still aimless. We set a time frame, but mostly it is still "someday".

Maybe you read about it, maybe you talk to someone about it. You may have even bought something. There are a lot of hope guitars out there gathering dust. But these actions are random and don't move us any closer to making a new reality.

Making a new reality—becoming a writer—requires executing plans. Plans are concrete actions we take to make the dream come true. Taking guitar lessons. Practicing most days. Being intentional about the songs you are learning. Identifying and taking the next steps even if you are unsure of a destination.

To make our dreams come true, we must plan and take action. We must put in the work. To become a writer after retirement, we can't just snap our fingers and be there.

One of my children dreamed of finding a job where he could work remotely and then move around and live in different cities and countries around the world. It sat in the dream state for a long time. The pandemic hit and forced him to work at home.

While the initial step was directly the result of the pandemic, the momentum took them from dream to hope. He has now camped at several places while working, enjoying some of the more spectacular parts of the United States. As of this writing, he is closer to making plans, not hopes, to live in another country while working remotely.

Another child flew through the dreams and hope stages for something more personal: tattoos. She started talking to me about getting a tattoo before her sixteenth birthday. She wasn't happy with the answer, but there definitely was a plan. On her eighteenth birthday, she was sitting in the tattoo chair. The design she chose was thoughtful, one she will never regret.

She had a plan and made it happen. In fact, several years later, the plan expanded to include a common tattoo with me. I'm not a tattoo guy for a variety of reasons, but when she proposed matching, thoughtful, tattoos, I had to say yes. And now we have matching tattoos. (Yes, I think it is really cool. No, I don't intend to get another one.)

Dreams. Hopes. Plans. There is nothing wrong with dreams that never make it to plans and reality. The image of me being a rock star is firmly cemented in the dream stage. I am ok with that.

The daydreams are fun and I know that the work is not something I am interested in doing.

When an idea is in the hope stage, it is a bit in limbo. More tangible than a dream, but without the direction and motion of a plan. This is where you decide you want to make the dream come true and start investigating what it will actually take. You might even take some action, but it isn't part of a plan.

You buy a guitar and a chord book, but don't practice much. You watch some videos on woodworking. You listen to some podcasts on how to be a writer.

Ideas float around in your head that are more concrete. More specific. You imagine yourself doing the work. But you don't start doing the work.

A plan is where you take action towards a goal. You sign up for guitar lessons and you practice frequently. You start using the woodworking tools to make things. You start writing consistently.

There is not a timeframe for any of this. Some dreams stay dreams forever. Some ideas skip the dream and hope stage and go right to plans. My wife is famous in our family for this. She seems to wake up one day with the plan formed and ready to go. When asked, no she hadn't been thinking about it for a while. She decided she was going to do the new thing, and she started doing it.

Where does writing sit for you? Is it a dream? A hope? A plan? Since you are reading this book, I would say it is at least a hope as you are taking action to make it a reality.

If you decide to make it into a plan, don't get burdened down by thinking it needs to be a complex plan that encompasses everything in this book. It doesn't.

A plan with one or two next steps on it is still a plan. The steps need to have a timeframe on them and need action. Saying "next year I will start" is not a plan, that is still a hope. Something like "I have started my practice document and I will write for five minutes a day at least three times a week" is a plan once you start.

Always have a plan. Make sure it is your plan, not somebody else's. Make sure it matches the level of effort you are willing and able to put in. It can be as simple and as complex as you want. If you feel you aren't a planner, at least know what your next step is, and keep moving forward.

The important part is taking action. If you want to turn writing into reality, you have to start. If you write, you are a writer. If you don't, you aren't.

Why Do You Want To Write?

People write for many reasons. You need to know what your reasons are. There are no wrong reasons, but there are wrong reasons for you. There are an infinite number of right reasons, but there will be only one or two right reasons for you.

Knowing why you want to be a writer will influence everything that you do on your journey. As we will see in the later parts of this book, your reasons will direct you to different craft, tool, and business decisions.

So let's look at some reasons people write. This is not a complete list (there is no such thing), but hopefully will give you some ideas. Remember, there are no wrong reasons.

- Write for yourself
- Write because you have things you want people to hear
- Write because you love books
- Write because you love writing
- Write to be creative
- Write to escape
- Write because you have to write
- Write to capture your life
- Write to capture someone else's life
- Write to capture history
- Write to be famous

- Write to make money
- Write to make change
- Write to discover what you believe
- Write to make sense of the world or events
- Write for mental relief
- Write to process a personal experience
- Write to connect to others
- Write to relax
- Write to entertain others
- Write to win awards
- Write for ego
- Write for status
- Write to teach
- Write to warn
- Write to bring ideas to life
- Write to influence
- Write to leave a legacy
- Write to entertain yourself
- Write for attention
- Write because you love words
- Write to experience life deeper

As you scan through the above list, here are a few questions that might help you understand why you want to write.

Who is your audience?

Do you want anyone other than yourself to read what you write?

Think of a set of ever-growing circles with you in the center. You are your first audience member. Maybe close family or friends is the next circle out. Your local community next. There might be certain groups you want to write for. The last circle is everyone on the planet. There can be many circles in between.

The key to all this is that it takes more to move to the next circle out. More energy. More planning. More work. More money. More stress. More worry.

Writing for yourself? Easy. Write and read it.

Writing for family? This is harder as you have to share it in some fashion (PDF? Ebook? Stack of paper? Physical book?). You will want and get feedback that you need to be ready for. Or worse, you will get no feedback, only the sound of silence.

Community? Maybe sending it in to a local newspaper. Drawing attention from your neighbors.

Selling it on the internet? Wow, now you are talking about getting an editor, book cover designer, learning about advertisers, and so forth. Or not. Maybe you just publish it on your website for free and don't allow comments and don't track how many people read it.

Want it in bookstores everywhere? You need to learn about all the different ways to get it into physical and ebook stores. Learn about aggregators, distributers, print-on-demand, and so forth.

Want to sell lots of copies of your book? How good are you at self-promotion? Social media? Many of us were raised not to brag about our work. Promoting ourselves is uncomfortable. But you simply can't sell books without self-promotion. For some, the discomfort is so intense they back away from selling their books. Unfortunately, the Opponent wins quite often in this area.

While independent publishing has made reaching a wider audience much easier, it is still work to move to the outer circles. The mechanics of publishing are easier (no gatekeepers!), but you still have to write the book, publish it, and make people aware of it.

To choose your audience, start at the inner circle (writing for yourself) and go out one ring at a time. Remember that each line will take more work. It will expose you to feedback from others and you will have more chances of not doing as well as you hoped.

The circle you end on will help you understand the audience you want to write for. Note that this will change over time. You may start out only for yourself or family and someday move further out. That's ok, there is no wrong way here.

Here is my answer to this question: My audience is the world. I want to write books that anyone on the planet might pick up and enjoy. I don't have an expectation that they will. After all, there is no style, genre, or type of writing that is universally liked, but that is my audience.

Since I am interested in both non-fiction and fiction, I have two sub-audiences. I worked in IT for my career and my non-fiction writing is aimed at others in IT. "People who work in IT" is a relatively small audience. I wrote this book for people retiring from any career to become writers. That is a larger potential audience than the IT books. I also plan to write fiction which is an even larger potential audience.

Take some time to figure out who you want to write for. It will force you to think about why you are writing.

What do you hope to get out of writing?

Even if you are writing for an audience, the writer gets something out of the writing itself. The joy of creating. Money. Satisfaction of telling a good story?

Is it a personal and private thing for you? Are you writing to process a trauma? You might get all the benefits by writing something only you see. Are you writing to prove to yourself that you can?

Maybe you don't want to do the work of getting your writing published. You might be content writing books and having the satisfaction of having written them.

Maybe it is the buzz from someone else reading your work and changing their mind. Maybe it is money you hope to get. Maybe it is the fame of people knowing your name.

Maybe you already have writing skills, and you just want to make some side money writing for others. Copywriters and technical writers can make good money.

My writer friend says that she is great at promoting others but "horrible" at promoting herself. This is totally the Opponent talking. When you think about promoting yourself, the Opponent goes into overdrive to convince you that you aren't worthy of this promotion. We see our own internal mess and we see only the exterior of others. The Opponent takes advantage of this internal knowledge and pounds us over the head with it 24x7. It isn't easy, but fight back. We are better than we think we are and we are taking small steps to improve. The Opponent is the enemy. The Opponent is wrong. We are worthy of promoting.

> My friend says that she is great at promoting others but "horrible" at promoting herself. This is totally the Opponent talking. When you think about promoting yourself, the Opponent goes into overdrive to convince you that you aren't worthy of this promotion.

Your answer to this question (what do you hope to get out of writing?) may not be a singular one. There may be multiple reasons and they may change as you learn more. That's ok.

Don't judge any of the possible answers. There are far more possible answers than will apply to you. Judging what others want to get out of writing is a waste of your time, unproductive, and also makes you a bit of an ass. It is more important to identify what is important to you and let others do their own thing.

I enjoy writing and I get satisfaction out of what I create. I enjoy helping people learn new skills or grow in their career.

How much work do you want to put in?

This is a big question. I view retirement as no longer working a full-time job. I don't view retirement as not doing any work. Anyone that retires to woodworking, home projects, volunteering, etc. is signing up for work.

The difference is that it is work you want to do. Work that you enjoy. Work that you are doing for yourself and not someone else.

Remember the circles in the first question? I said that moving outward requires more work. Getting your work published or sold takes work. You need to get your book to market it and promote it. Moving outward in the circles means taking more risks by sharing your work with others and receiving more feedback (good and bad) about your work.

Whether you traditionally publish or publish independently, you must put the work in to make your book a reality. Traditional publishing means soliciting agents, editors, publishers to accept your book. Independent publishing means doing all the work yourself or paying for outside experts. This includes editing, book cover design, and making it available to physical and online bookstores.

You will also have to do the marketing yourself regardless of which path you take. Unless you are an already established writer, publishers will expect you to do the heavy lifting on marketing.

How much money do you want to invest?

Like almost anything else you choose to do in retirement, writing costs money. You can get by cheap if you write on paper and never share it with anyone. Most other writing will cost you something.

Here are some things that you may end of spending money on. Costs will vary widely, so I am not including any specifics. You may not need all of these depending on your plan.

- A computer.

- A place to store and backup electronic files (Google Drive, Apple Cloud, Microsoft OneDrive, spare hard drives, etc.).

- Software tools for writing and formatting.

- A website. First you need a domain (for example, johnbredesen.com). The domain is your address on the internet, so don't get fancy. Make it easy to remember and type. Second, you need the website itself. There are many services available that make it easy to do this.

- An editor

- A book cover designer

- An illustrator

- Buying personal copies of your books.

- Advertising

If you get a traditional publishing deal, the publisher may cover the costs of the editor, cover designer, and illustrator.

If you want to sell your writing, you must treat it like a business. New businesses take investments. There will be the opportunity to choose levels of spending for most the above items. You will get to choose how much you will spend, but you absolutely will need to spend money if you intend to make money from your work.

With these questions and the above list, you should be able to take a first crack at why you are writing.

Why does this matter? Why is it important that you know why you are writing? We don't need a reason to write, do we? We can just write for the enjoyment of it and not get all tangle up in this reason crap. Right?

Maybe? Maybe not?

If you are writing just for yourself and will not share it with anyone, you probably don't need this chapter, indeed, you probably don't need this book. (Although I think it might have some useful tips even for that situation.)

But here we are and I'm guessing that you want others to read your work, and probably want to put it out there into the world for people to buy.

Why Am I Writing?

So what is my answer to this question? This took me a bit to figure out.

Did I want to publish a book with my name on it? Yes. Did I want to be a New York Times bestseller? Meh. Sure, it would be nice, but that didn't feel like a goal for me. Did I want to win awards? I might enter a contest here and there, but, no, winning awards was not a goal to work towards.

Did I want to make money from writing? Yes, but since I had retirement income, I didn't need my writing to pay all the bills.

So I started with the following goals.

1. Make beer money. This is shorthand for making a bit more money than I was spending. In business terms, I wanted my writing to be profitable.

2. Publish at least one book. Interestingly, while preparing for retirement, I already hit this goal. So when I actually retired, I updated the book count goal. This is my third book after a second IT leadership book. I think I will be able to write multiple fiction books when I move on from non-fiction.

My new goal became "I will be a profitable, multi-series author."

Unfortunately, I can only control one of the two goals. I can write and publish the books, but I have little control over people buying them. I intend to do ads and other marketing, but there is no guarantee the sales will come.

So why am I writing? My goal only tells part of the story. In their books on writing, both Steven Pressfield and Elizabeth Gilbert both make the point that if we don't enjoy the process of writing, we are doing it wrong. As I practiced more, writing more fiction stories and publishing my non-fiction books, it became clear that I enjoy the process of writing.

I enjoy sitting down and figuring out characters and story. I like writing chapters that tell my career journey in a way that helps others. I like the writing part of being an author.

Sure, it isn't all kittens and roses. Sometimes it is really hard to figure out how to organize a section. Some contests I entered really stumped me. Sometimes it was a slog to get through a section that I knew wasn't good enough, but I didn't know how to make it better. Sometimes the tedium of editing would make me scream (literally, in a few cases).

But, overall, I concluded that, yes, I enjoyed writing enough to continue it, regardless of the world's acceptance or rejection. This was the last step to knowing that I had made a good choice for my retirement.

Am I Good Enough?

I was talking with a friend of mine a few months ago about my writing. A bunch of friends were over, and he and I were sitting out on the deck, beers in hand, enjoying the crisp fall day. He asked me an interesting question: *Some people just aren't very good at writing. How do you know you are good enough?*

I didn't have a good answer. It was one of those situations where I knew I *should* have the answer, but I didn't. I mumbled something about building confidence and then, to my relief, others wandered out to the deck and the conversation moved elsewhere.

His question stuck in my head. I have heard it from others since then, maybe because I was listening for it. I also heard variations of it from the other side—people who wanted to be an author and didn't know if they were good enough. I've heard from a few where that question prevented them from even starting down the writing path.

There isn't some test you can take where you get a score (634 out of 950 points!) that you can compare to other writers. Could you imagine if there was? There would be study guides, practice tests, and tutors. Pressure from parents. Some would brag. Some would cry.

Writers who are unsure of themselves (which, to be clear, is ALL OF US!) would find all sorts of anxiety in our scores and strive mightily to improve them. Or give up. That sounds more like a horror story (hmmm... let me write that idea in my journal). No, I don't think an objective test would be a good thing at all.

The question still lingered. Am I good enough?

Maybe book sales is the measure. The number of books you sell as the definitive sign of how good you are as a writer. Hmmm, don't think I like that one either. There is too much that is simply out of our control. Popularity is not a good indicator of quality. More importantly, there is a lot of good writing that never sees the light of day for lots of reasons.

How many people don't develop their writing because they receive no or negative support when they first tried? How many people would be good writers but they didn't grow up in a household that gave them the opportunity? How many Mozarts have we missed because they had no musical instrument in the house? Or if they did, they never got a recording contract because no one ever knew? Or they became well known in their community, but their community wasn't plugged into the larger music scene.

> Count the people with writing talent that never write a book. Count the people who write a book that isn't very good. The first number is orders of magnitude bigger than the second.

Count the people with writing talent that never write a book. Count the people who write a book that isn't very good. The first number is orders of magnitude bigger than the second.

My starting point to an answer is this: you won't know if you are good enough until you write something. Anything else is speculation. If you spend a lot of time speculating instead of writing, you will never know the answer.

You have to start somewhere. You have to start writing.

Now starting to write doesn't answer my friend's question, but at least you will find out where you are. You may find out you are decent and have some natural talent. That would be awesome.

But chances are, you will be ok. Not great. Not terrible. That's where I am. That's where many people are.

However, writing is not a single monolithic skill. Just like any art form, there are many different skills that make up writing. You might be good at romance dialogue but not battle scene dialogue. You might be good at describing a forest, but not a busy street.

We will be good in some parts, bad in some, and ok in most. You won't know until you try. My approach is to find one thing I am good at and then build from there. If you are writing what you like to read, then you have a nice situation where (1) you like what you write, and (2) there is a part of it you are good at. Building on that is straightforward.

I had gotten some positive feedback on certain parts of my writing from my wife and from the writing group. This helped me to understand where to start. I built on that and slowly expanded the areas that I was good at, at least according to me and my very small writing group.

All this solidified my plan to publish independently. I couldn't know if I was any good as a writer until I put my work out there and let people decide to spend their money on my work.

It is like running a marathon. We can do all the practice runs we want, but until we enter one to see what our real time is, we wouldn't know if we were any good. Even then, *good* is usually defined by the time we were aiming for instead of a certain place in the standings.

We would learn so much from that first marathon. We would know if we crossed the finish line (shipped our book). We can compare our time to what we wanted (satisfaction with our book). We would know if we wanted to do another one. We would have an idea on how we could train better for the next one (improve our book writing process).

Maybe you are a one book and done person. Awesome. Many people run just one marathon as a personal goal and have no desire to run another one (write another book). Maybe you want to run one more (write another book). Maybe you already know you want to run lots of marathons (write lots of books) like a friend of mine whose goal it is to run a marathon in every state (ok, too many parentheses here—you get the point).

To be clear, I have never run a marathon and have no desire to. I ran cross-country in high school and was happy to stop when I graduated. I am in awe of people that dedicate themselves to the effort of running 26 plus miles.

I am also in awe of anyone who writes a book. I may not know what it is like to run a marathon, but I know the effort it takes to write a book. Completing and shipping a book is an accomplishment to be proud of.

Worrying about being good shouldn't get in the way. Focus on finishing and improving, and the "good enough" question takes care of itself.

Keep calm and keep improving.

So here is my answer to my friend's question.

> Keep calm and keep improving.

The definition of *good* is subjective. I have an opinion about my work. My wife has an opinion. My writing group has an opinion. If I am only writing for myself, that's good enough. Am I good enough to sell lots of books? I won't know unless I publish.

I worked in IT for most of my career, however, I worked outside of IT for about eight years. When you work in IT, the people in the company *have* to use your work. They can only use the internal systems that IT provides. I wanted to work in product development where outside customers would choose to use our products.

My decision to publish independently was a similar decision. I wanted to put my books out on the market and see if people would choose to spend their own money to buy them. If I traditionally published, I have to get past the gatekeepers before my book hits the market. If I independently published, I can put my book out there myself.

Selling books is a big complicated thing and there are lots of reasons that people won't buy my books, the primary one being that they don't know about them. But they can't buy them if they aren't on the market.

You may have heard the quote by Theodore Roosevelt. It comes from a speech he gave while on a European tour in 1910, after his US Presidency had ended.

> *It is not the critic who counts; not the man who points out how the strong man stumbles, or where the doer of deeds could have done them better. The credit belongs to the man who is actually in the arena, whose face is marred by dust and sweat and blood; who strives valiantly; who errs, and comes short again and again, because there is no effort without error and shortcoming; but who does actually strive to do the deeds; who knows the great enthusiasms, the great devotions; who spends himself in a worthy cause;*

who at the best knows in the end the triumph of high achievement, and who at the worst, if he fails, at least fails while daring greatly, so that his place shall never be with those cold and timid souls who know neither victory nor defeat.
  - Theodore Roosevelt

I think this quote carries truth. There are those (of any gender) that do and those that criticize. Criticism is easy and takes very little effort compared to the effort of writing a story of any length. It isn't friends, acquaintances, or even readers that will decide if you are any good. It is only you. If you like writing and are getting what you hoped for from writing, then you are a success.

Be a doer of deeds.

We Will Get Better, a.k.a. Continuous Improvement

One of the Opponent's lies is to tell us that our writing is not good enough. The story lines have all been done. The characters are flat. The dialogue would bore a hyperactive squirrel to sleep.

The challenge is that, when we start to write, the Opponent is kind of right. When we first start to write, our tentative first steps won't be very good. The trick is to understand that our Opponent is saying this with the goal of getting us to quit. But a simple twist of the situation can provide motivation.

I was fortunate to have people around me that supported the idea of retiring to writing. My wife, Joyce, was only positive, and I appreciated that. The writing group gave me positive feedback.

But even with her support, it was hard to show Joyce my writing. When you start writing, the Opponent makes it hard to show anyone. I knew I wanted her to be my first reader, so I had to take that step.

Showing my work to her, of course, didn't cause the world to end or cause me horrendous embarrassment. She was encouraging.

Now one other person had seen my fiction. It was a small step in the right direction.

There is a concept in business called Continuous Improvement. If the culture of an organization is one of continuous improvement, then there are always projects, big and small, that make the organization better. The belief is that, no matter how bad we are today, we can be better tomorrow.

> No matter how bad we are today, we can be better tomorrow.

I lived this concept throughout my work career, and it has been useful as I work into my writing career. I wrote a blog post ("Yeah, I suck, but I'll get better…") that covers this. It was before the idea of the Opponent had become clear to me, but you can see bits of the idea in the post.

The simple twist is this. The Opponent says "You suck, you should quit." I say "I suck, but I will get better." One is defeatist. One is forward looking with a continuous improvement mindset. This mindset makes a world of difference.

We should look at other people's writing as examples to aspire to or examples to learn from. We should not look at them as comparisons.

If you read something you really like, and your thoughts run to "I could never write something this good, I should just give up," the Opponent is in your head again. If you read a bit of writing that immerses you in a situation or tears your heart out or makes you laugh until you have tears, mark it. Highlight the passage. Go back to it and learn from it. Figure out what words and sentence structure made you feel like you did.

Don't let the Opponent use great writing to diminish our own writing. Use great writing to lift your writing higher.

Here are some ideas.

- Turn on all spell and grammar checkers. Now, I'll grant you that the little squiggly lines under the words can be annoying. They can distract you from the sentence you are trying to type. They interrupt your flow. But if you learn to avoid making those mistakes in the first place, you end up writing cleaner copy and saving yourself time and money during editing. This is a long-term/short-term thing. It is distracting short-term, but learning how to prevent the squigglies is an important long-term skill.

- Transcribe a passage from a book you really like. The act of moving those words through your brain will help you understand how the author created the scene and the emotions. Try to do it with authors of different styles.
- Internet Videos can be a source of good (and bad) advice on writing.
- Some podcasts, like *Writing Excuses*, have writing assignments. Work through those.

I recommend having a plan for where you are improving. Working on one or two improvements at a time helps you make sure the improvement sticks. It doesn't matter how small the improvements are, or how many. What matters is that you are continuously improving.

Our physical condition

While there are many benefits to being retirement age, the list probably does not include our physical body. Like putting miles on a car, our body has done much for us over the years and we don't always take care of it like we should.

Don't underestimate the impact of physical condition on your writing. Being our age isn't the bundle of pain-free joy we wish it was. I won't bore you with all the benefits of exercise, as you have heard them for years. It probably had as much impact on you as it did on me: minimal.

The rude truth is that, at our age, our physical condition is going downhill. In our youth, exercise made us healthier and more in shape. Now, exercise keeps us from getting worse. Remember two things: Doing something is better than doing nothing. And doing a little bit more today than yesterday is a good thing.

There is too much talk about what is the best workout. About the latest workout product advertised on late night TV. About the best exercise technique. The unending search for the *perfect* exercise gets in the way of doing *something*.

Ignore the internet's advice. Ignore your family's advice. Ignore your friends' advice. Or rather, listen, but decide for yourself. Doing something, no matter how little, is better than doing nothing. The best exercise program is the one you follow.

If you did something yesterday (or last week or last month), doing a little bit more today (or this week or this month) is progress. Like with your writing, only compare yourself with yourself, not with anyone else.

Did you do something physical today?

Did you do a little bit more than last week?

Don't make a big plan, unless that is how you work best. Don't sign up for new stuff, unless that is how you work best. Don't buy the latest exercise gadget, unless that is how you work best. We shouldn't try to fool ourselves, though. At our age, if we haven't done it before, the chances of us starting a big new habit is unlikely. Start with small steps.

Of course, if you have existing pains that getting in better shape won't help, don't make it worse. If you have a bad hip that will need replacing some day, focus on your core, upper body, and arms. Ditto for the shoulders or back, do something with the other parts. Be smart.

Your chair and desk matter. I could only write for about 90 minutes before my butt and back started talking to me. Turns out I need arms on my chair. Helps my posture. My work chair always had arms, but my home one didn't and that caused me problems.

Your attention span may be an issue. It takes mental energy to write. It is hard for the most prolific writers to write for more than a few hours straight at a time. I could only write for about 20 minutes at the beginning before my attention started wandering. As you increase your writing time, you will discover you need to take breaks to let the story continue to develop in your head or to figure out a plot point. Or to just take a physical break and walk around a bit, maybe take the dog for a walk.

Typing speed matters. As you get better and the stories are going from your brain to the keyboard, your fingers will be the bottleneck. As the story unrolls in your brain, you will struggle to type fast enough. Spending a little time on improving your typing speed will pay off in the long run. If you have hand issues, you might consider a different keyboard or learning to dictate instead of typing.

Spouses & Partners

Writing advice books rarely address spouses and partners. Perhaps it's because their spouse still works and writing is their full-time job. Perhaps it is because they are single. Either way, retiring into a writing career has some special issues that come up if you have a spouse or partner.

If this doesn't apply to you, go ahead and skip this chapter.

I bring this topic up because this is still a work in progress for Joyce and me. We are both transitioning to retirement and working through some of these issues. There is, of course, no answer that works for all couples. Each couple has to find their own path.

The concept of retirement is changing. When employees worked an entire career at one company, retirement meant leaving the only company they knew. Retirement meant that an employee was all done working. As employees became more mobile, it is rare to stay with one company for an entire career.

There are three questions we have asked over the years that I think are really the same. In high school or college, people asked us "What are you going into?" or "What are you studying?". In our working years, in a semi-serious way, we would say things like "I'm trying to figure out what I want to do when I grow up" when facing a job or possible career change. And now at our age, we wonder what we will do after we retire.

These are all variations of "What's next in my life?" It is never a permanent decision, it is only the next thing. Retirement is that milestone where we stop working full time for others, and, hopefully, start working for ourselves.

You have decided that writing will be part of that answer.

I want to talk about what happens when we retire specifically to become a writer. Presuming we have a plan in place, we will need to spend some time each day, or at least some days, working on our writing. This is time spent by ourselves mentally, if not physically. Writing is not usually a communal task. You can't have another person actively involved in your writing. It isn't like working on a garden or home improvement project where working together makes sense.

Writing is a solitary task. We need to do it by ourselves. We may be physically in the same room as someone else, but we are mentally far away. What is the other person doing during this time? Deciding to be a writer means that both of you need to have solitary tasks. If you don't, the other person will want to do something together when you want to write.

> Writing is a solitary task. We need to do it by ourselves. We may be physically in the same room as someone else, but we are mentally far away. What is the other person doing during this time?

This means that your decision to be a writer has a direct impact on your spouse or partner. This impact is more than just taking another job. Retirement adds expectations of being together and spending more time together. A plan to be a writer is pressure in the other direction.

Let me put a finer point on this. You can't be a writer unless the other person in your relationship also has a plan to do something by themselves while you are writing.

Unlike changing jobs, retirement has the connotation of less work or being done with work. Our plan to become a writer needs to take that into account. Are we going to go at being a writer with the same intensity that we had when working? Will we put in a full workday? Or will we put in fewer hours? If so, how many?

Our answer will have a big impact on our retirement. If we intend to be a full-time writer, working a full workday, then we are really just changing jobs. Sure, we might financially be retired, drawing on our retirement resources, but our days will be full of doing a specific job.

Becoming a full-time writer after retirement is no different than changing jobs as far as our spouse or partner is concerned. We will schedule our days to be full of writing, editing, publishing, marketing, promoting, etc.

The flip side is if you make no time commitment to becoming a writer. If you want to leave your days completely free and write when you want. This is a perfectly legitimate plan. But if you look at the two options—writing full time and not having any plan to write—you can see that those are the bookends of all possible choices. You will make the most progress by writing full time and you will make the least progress by not having any plan.

So, like it or not, if you have a high desire to become a writer and published author, you must decide how many hours a day you will spend on it. One? Four? Six? Remember that if you don't have a plan, you are still in the dream or hope stage and writing will remain always in the future.

Retirement Timing

Timing of retirement is also a factor. Either you both retire at the same time or one of you is retiring before the other.

Let's first look at retiring one at a time. When this happens, one person is still going to work every day, and the other isn't. Imagine a couple: Chris and Taylor. Let's say that Chris is retiring and Taylor is still working. Taylor still gets up and does their job, worrying about work schedule, vacation, etc. Chris is now retired and plans to be a writer.

While Taylor is working, Chris can figure out a new schedule and useful habits. They talk in the morning and evening. The days aren't really much different from before Chris retired. From a relationship perspective, Chris just got a new job.

When one person retires first, there are two transitions: when the first person retires and then when the second person retires. The challenge comes when the second person retires. Chris is in a routine and Taylor needs to create one. It is a safe bet to say that Chris' routine will have to change to accommodate Taylor's.

Taylor has it a little easier as the new habits will already take Chris into account. But Chris might have a harder time adjusting to a new person crowding in on time and space. Some of it will be good, some might need to be worked through.

When two people hope to retire at the same time, each of you are creating new habits. The existence of the other will heavily influence each habit. Both of you are trying to work out a new focus and schedule.

It will take a while to figure out the new routine. There are so many options and possibilities for retirement. There can be too much freedom, too many options, which can lead to a longer transition time.

Creating the new retirement habit, or habits, is also complicated by the transition time. When you change to a new job, the job directs your schedule and habits. When you retire, there is no outside force influencing you. You have to figure it out for yourself. Or yourselves, in this case.

There will be a transition time from your last day of work until you feel like there is a new routine, however loose, in place.

The first few weeks of retirement are like a staycation, a vacation where you stay at home. You may have a few things planned, maybe a trip, maybe some house projects. In the end, the full work day you used to have is gone, and you need to fill those hours with something. Work is no longer hanging over your head.

My Transition

I retired a few months before my wife did. So I started my retirement transition first. I had grand hopes of writing a certain amount each day.

My initial writing plan was an hour in the morning when I am mentally freshest, and then a couple more hours during the day or evening. That didn't work as planned. Often the only writing was that initial hour. But it was interesting how many things there were to do now that I had weekdays to do them. There seemed to always be errands to run and things to fix.

Also our morning coffee, which had been about 20-30 minutes when we both worked, became 60-90 minutes when I didn't have to leave for the office.

We didn't easily slide into a new routine, as there always seemed to be something unique about the day. In fact, here we are six months later and we still don't have a set schedule.

One of our retirement goals is to make time for physical activity. We are getting older and need to put the care into keeping our bodies from fading too fast. Aging brings physical decline, so it is really figuring out how to fight a holding pattern.

Adding physical activity to our schedule complicates things. Neither of us does well with physical activity using only self-motivation. We have joined the local YMCA and are using their classes. They only offered those classes at certain times so that influences our calendar. The other complicating factor is that the classes that are right for us are not every day. This means that our daily schedule won't be the same. I know this will be a challenge for my writing routine.

Before retiring, the closest thing to retirement a couple experiences is vacation. Trips to places you want to see. Trips to see kids and grandkids. Trips to see extended family or friends. Actual vacations where you stay at home with nothing planned (a.k.a. staycation) are rare.

I think there are three kinds of time a retired couple face.

1. Time together doing the same activity. Think coffee in the morning, projects, movies, cleaning, errands, walking in the park, going to a museum, and so forth. These are shared experiences.

2. Time together doing different activities. Think reading, crafting, watching TV, writing, and so forth. These are separate activities that might occur in the same room, allowing interaction.

3. Time doing different activities in separate locations. Think volunteering. part-time jobs, lunch with friends, and so forth.

There are certain times of the day that Joyce and I connect. The first is morning coffee. Our conversation is wide ranging from today's schedule to the various body aches we woke up with (remember: old) to camping plans to our kids to solving the world's problems. The days we miss that are hard.

We also have dinner together, which lets us discuss the day. Since we built this habit over our years together, the conversation always contained a bit about work. As we move into retirement, I think the things we do independently will replace work.

One of our particular challenges is travel. We have a motorhome and hope to travel around the country. We both want to do that. The issue is what we do when we get to a place. I want to write when we are traveling. I know that if I can't write while on the road, I won't want to travel.

So I want to write while traveling. That means sitting at the campsite with my computer and writing. That means climbing into my head to write stories. I wrote part of this book at a campground just outside of Nashville.

Joyce, on the other hand, wants to see things. If we go to a new place, she wants to see the sites. Explore the interesting places. Try the fun restaurants. Hear the music. However, when we are at state parks, she loves to hang at the campsite or go for hikes.

So when we plan our trips, we need to balance hanging at the campsite and seeing things. Related to that is how structured a trip is. Do we have assigned site-seeing days and designated hang at the campsite days? How does weather factor in? This is something we will need to figure out and I imagine it will take a year or two to find our groove.

Together & Separate

A couple's relationship is healthier when we are also connected with the outside world. I'm not talking about TV or newspapers.

I'm talking about being out in the world, doing things without each other. Volunteering at different places, joining an organization related to your interests, anything that has each of you interacting with the outside world. Separately.

There are several benefits when the couple, as individuals, are interacting with the outside world. First is the obvious, to me at least, fact that two people cannot spend 24 hours a day together without a break. Every couple needs time apart.

I'm sure you have heard the conversations about introverts and extraverts. None of us are 100% one or the other. All of us have some level of introvert and need time by ourselves. Whether this is time we spend writing or doing something else, it is important to make sure that each person gets their alone time. If there is a big difference in the amount of alone time needed, at least get it out in the open and talk about it.

> *I'm sure you have heard the conversations about introverts and extraverts. None of us are 100% one or the other. All of us have some level of introvert and need time by ourselves.*

To be honest, *I* don't want to spend 24 hours a day with *me*, I can't imagine anyone else wanting to. The important thing to remember is this need for some amount of alone time has *nothing* to do with the other person. Taylor needs time alone just because of Taylor—it has nothing to do with Chris. And vice versa. So don't take it personally when your partner needs alone time. You need it too. Taking it personally is wrong and counterproductive.

Second, having time apart gives each person a chance to talk about their day. I believe these conversations are how a couple stays connected. By doing things separately, each has something to share with the other. This one was, ok *is*, harder for me. I wasn't one to talk about the specifics of what I did, especially my writing. But Joyce was curious, and I wanted to share.

This kind of communication can be different. Joyce has no problem talking about her day and I love hearing about it. But when I try to talk about my day, I have a problem. I wanted to share, but I sucked at it.

When I would start talking about my writing session, my brain would race ahead, heading down bunny trails, thinking about my writing. Something I need to add to my current book. The tasks for tomorrow. Whatever. I would forget to talk. I would stop talking in the middle of a sentence or just trail off. Joyce would think that I didn't want to talk. She didn't know what was going on in my head—I just stopped talking. So she would stop asking questions. That one took us a couple of months to figure out. Once I realized I was thinking ahead of my mouth, I could work on reducing the bunny trails and staying in the conversation.

When you think about your time in retirement with a spouse or partner, think about the following table. We know that writing is an activity that is done separately. Talking through the table can help you both get on the same page.

	Together	Separate
How much time together?	_____	_____
What Activities?	_____ _____	Writing _____

Questions for couples to ask themselves

- How much time do we expect to spend together? When we retire, we will be able to spend more time together. Awesome! The thought of spending every minute of every day with the other person? Perhaps not so awesome. Between the extremes of zero and spending every waking moment with each other, what feels like a good range? Days will vary and this won't be an exact recipe. Presumably, you will want to spend more time with each other than before retirement. But if one of you wants to spend most of the day together and the other wants to put the time into being a writer, you can see where there might be conflict.

- When the writer is writing, what will the other person do? If they are sitting around waiting for the writer to finish, that just adds to the pressure the writer facing. *Remember that Taylor is waiting for you to finish, so why don't you just stop now?*

- What do you want your days to look like? Will they be completely unstructured? Will there be a schedule? Your personalities will decide that. But the plan to be a writer will, by necessity, require that there be some structure. How is that worked into the day? For example, even though I am not getting up for an outside job, I still have an alarm set so that I can get my early morning writing time in. Some of you may rebel against the idea of any alarm after retirement. Each couple needs to find their own path.

- What does retirement mean to each of you? It means no longer working in your career jobs. You will need to work through things like travel, projects, meals, and so forth. Is there a part-time job? Is there volunteering? Whatever the two of you decide, having the conversation is important.

Chapter 5: Writing Non-Fiction

Remember, Teach, Learn
Many reasons to write down
Your unique lifetime

As I mentioned earlier, I have already written and published two non-fiction books. This book is my third. In this chapter, I will cover what I learned writing and publishing them.

Non-fiction was not my original plan. My goal is to write fiction, and I had started down that path. But I was new to the whole writing thing, and when the stall came (it always comes—the Opponent never quits), the idea of writing a non-fiction book popped in.

I had spent decades in the IT business, most of them in a leadership position. This gave me a wealth of knowledge and perspective on the topic. I also had strong opinions on how to manage an IT department. Maybe I could write a book for IT Leaders?

Joanna Penn (see "Resources") has a book out called *How to Write Non-Fiction*. She covers a wide variety of topics that I find very helpful, especially the chapter titled *Can I Write A Book If I'm Not An Expert?* I strongly recommend her book if you are interested in writing non-fiction.

I ended up writing two non-fiction books for IT Leaders. The first, *The IT Leaders' Handbook* (referred to from here on out as *Handbook*) was targeted at the experienced IT leader. The second, *The IT Leader's First Days* (referred to as *First Days*), was aimed at the brand new IT Leader.

This chapter will be a combination of the story of writing these two books along with important things I learned that might be helpful to others.

Writing My First Non-Fiction Book

I had read lots of non-fiction over the years, so I had some idea of what I liked and what I didn't. However, as I sat down to write *Handbook*, this reading experience didn't help me write. Since I hadn't written a book before, I didn't have a good idea for how to organize the chapters. There seemed to be a bit of *chicken & egg* between the words and the order of the chapters. Oh well, when all else fails, just start writing.

I didn't have an outline when I started. I created chapters about topics I wanted to talk about and added more chapters as I wrote. Interestingly, as I got into the writing, I became better at identifying things during my workday that would be helpful in the book.

After I had written almost two dozen chapters, I realized the organization was a mess. I wrote the name of each chapter on a piece of paper and spread them out on the dining room table. Moving them around, I came up with the organization the book needed.

The organization allowed me to present a narrative that flowed better than the random chapters. My past reading had given me an idea of how these types of books should flow, and I found the right one for my content.

I wrote the book over several months. Some sections came easy. Some did not. Eventually, most of the planned chapters had something in them. I printed it out and took a read through it.

Wow, what a mess.

Perhaps you have heard the phrase "finding your voice." Perhaps you know it as "writing style." Whatever we call it, I had a bunch of them. It was like different people had written different sections. Serious John. Casual John. Professor John. Manager John. Com-

> *Perhaps you have heard the phrase "finding your voice." Perhaps you know it as "writing style." Whatever we call it, I had a bunch of them.*

passionate John. Hardass John. There was even Drunk John as I wrote one section with the help of a bottle of wine. As an experiment. No, it wasn't my morning writing session, it was in the evening — there are limits to my experimentation.

Some chapters were very short and to the point. Some used humor. Some were a little longer and did a better job explaining. Some were written to an experienced reader, some were written to a novice reader. Some had stories. Some had quotes.

I like the word *style* better than the word *voice*. The style of my first draft varied wildly from chapter to chapter and I needed to settle on one style. Reading through the whole book showed me which style felt better. From there, I decided my target audience would be experienced IT people, and that stories helped illustrate my point.

So my first edit pass was cleaning up my style and bringing a more consistent feel to the book. This was really hard for me and took about six months. There were far too many days where I just stared at the screen, not knowing how to fix what I wrote. Sometimes I didn't bother fixing and just wrote another chapter on the same topic from scratch.

Through this, I realized that there were several chapters I needed to add. These were topics I had mentioned briefly, but were worthy of exploring in more detail. I also realized that there were some bigger ideas that didn't fit this book. Those got moved into my notes for another book on my To-Write list.

It was during this time that I came across the concept of a boneyard from Howard Taylor in the *Writing Excuses* podcast. While the word has been around for a long time, I had first heard it in the context of storing retired aircraft. The concept in writing is you don't delete larger chunks of text, but rather you move them to a document or section called Boneyard. By keeping these chunks around, you might find a use for it later. And it feels a lot better than deleting.

I went through several editing passes. I would print out the manuscript and use a red pen to make notes. Then I would apply those notes back to the manuscript. This was not very fun, and I struggled with motivation during this time. Sometimes all I was doing was putting in the time. When I didn't like a particular section or didn't know how to deal with it, my routine (writing between 5am-6am every weekday) forced me to do something — either edit the words I had or write new words. I found that eventually a tough passage would snap into clarity or a rewrite would feel much better.

Forcing myself to keep moving forward got me through days that I didn't know what I was going to do next. After all, writers write. Every author I had read about or listened to talked about the bad days. The days where nothing was going right, where the Opponent's voice was very loud in your head, where you got stuck on a section or you didn't know how to fix a chapter. But they all repeated the same point: keep pushing forward, don't give up.

> *Forcing myself to keep moving forward got me through days that I didn't know what I was going to do next.*

Now, beating my head against a wall for hours and hours was not productive. If something wasn't working, there were a few times when I set it aside and moved to another section. The front and back matter were favorite escape sections. Often, my subconscious would figure out a way through whatever mess I was working on, and the next writing session was better.

It certainly wasn't the plan, but the bulk of the writing and editing of the first book happened during the pandemic. Staying at home evenings and weekends made it easier to put the time in. My wife had some projects of her own, so she would do her thing and I would do my thing, usually in the same room.

My enthusiasm for the project came and went several times during these months. Fortunately, it was during this time that I came across several books and podcasts about the importance of not giving up. The importance of putting one foot in front of the other. Even a small footstep forward in the face of the Opponent's constant and terrible headwinds was still a step forward.

And the days when the steps went backwards? Those days required faith in myself. Faith that, when I got up the next morning and kept fighting, that I would eventually get through it. There were some mornings that I didn't get up and I came close to giving up. It came back to this: is writing a dream, a hope, or a plan? My answer was always *plan*, so I needed to keep going.

And I did.

Alpha Readers

Eventually I got within sight of completing what felt like a real first draft of the book. Or at least a draft that was worthy of showing other people.

But who?

Joyce was willing to read it, but she wasn't part of the intended audience. Same for my writing group. I had read a few sections to them and they gave me good feedback, but they couldn't speak as part of the intended audience.

The term *alpha readers* came from my experience with software development. After the software developers have written and tested a new piece of software, they will often use people outside the development team, called *beta testers*, to test the software in a wider range of uses. Occasionally, there is the need to test things before development is done and those testers are called *alpha testers*.

I needed someone to read my non-fiction book and tell me if it was something that IT professionals would be interested in. I needed to find *alpha readers*.

I reached out to some former colleagues in the IT business to see if they would be willing to participate. I sent them an email with the outline and introduction and asked if they would be willing to read the manuscript and give me feedback. I emphasized I was looking for higher-level feedback, not typos and commas.

I got the emails written, and the Opponent kicked into high gear. I hadn't told many folks that I was writing a book and here I was asking my peers to tell me what they think. These were people I looked up to. People I had learned from for years. I didn't know how they would respond and my Opponent filled in that gap with all kinds of discouraging thoughts and fears.

It took three days from the time I had the emails ready to when I was mentally able to click the send button. Three days of agonizing over wording and spelling and tone and all sorts of other things that probably didn't matter. Three days before I could take that step. Looking back, it was a small step, but it felt large. Eventually I clicked send.

Then I waited.

The first response came a day later, but it seemed like weeks. Fortunately, it was positive. I had my first alpha reader! I read the email calmly and closed it. Ha! Not really. I'm sure the neighbors heard the yell of excitement and there may have been dancing.

A few more responded positively and eventually I had a nice group of alpha readers. I sent out the *Handbook* manuscript with a deadline a month out. I also sent it to my editor with the same deadline.

Editor

Yup, I had an editor. All the learning I had done to that point had stressed the importance of having an editor, whether traditionally or independently published.

In my career, I had come across people who were editors. These people could be magical in their ability to improve other people's writing or they could be horrific and change it into an unrecognizable mess.

All of us have seen bad editing, perhaps in the news, perhaps in instruction manuals, perhaps in all the paperwork we have to read for insurance, doctors, the DMV, etc.

In the writing world, I think editors are mostly a force for good. Early writers (that's us!) need editors to teach us to be better storytellers as well as fix a specific story. In fairness, there are established authors who believe that editors don't help at all.

I learned about two primary types of editors. Development editors help you write a good book. Copyeditors help you write a book well. There are other types of editors that you may use as you get further down the writing journey, but these are the two to start with.

Development editors look at a piece of writing from a high level. Organization, flow, and logical progression for non-fiction. For fiction, editors help with character development and consistency, plot lines and holes, and maintaining reader interest. Development editors don't care about typos or awkward sentences unless they are too many and they get in the way of basic reading.

A development editor can be helpful at the start of a writer's career. Not only is our first book much better, but we will learn how to get the bigger things correct. You will find differing opinions from established writers. Some feel the development editor is best considered a teacher that you eventually won't need. Some feel that you should have faith in your own storytelling style and avoid development editors.

The idea of learning from a development editor seems to make the most sense to me. As I mentioned before, it is important to learn how to write clean the first time through. By becoming a better storyteller, my initial pass on the story will get better. I'm not to the point where I don't need a development editor, but I am learning with each book.

Copyeditors pay attention to grammar, typos, sentence structure. They make sure your paragraphs flow. They look at references. They look at awkward phrasing. Copyeditors are experts in the language and know the various rules and style books. They like reading a manuscript and marking the places where it can be better.

You will always have a copyeditor. Even as you improve, you will need someone who reads through for typos. There are always typos. You will come across them even in the most popular books.

In fact, I came up with a rule about typos. The Bredesen Rule of Typos says that if you have N people reading for typos, as N gets bigger, the speed that the N+1 person finds a typo gets faster. If you have two people read a manuscript and you apply the fixes, the time it takes for the third person to find a typo is faster than the first person. It should be the opposite, but it isn't. A related part of this rule says that the more typos you fix, the more you accidentally introduce. Yet another argument for learning how to write cleanly on your first draft.

The relationship between an author and editor is important. The author owns the writing and all decisions about what edits to apply. Editors only make suggestions. The author is under no obligation to accept the edits. This really comes into play when a development editor makes suggestions about organization and tone (non-fiction) or characters, dialogue, and plot (fiction). These are usually major changes and we need to believe it will make the book better before we make it.

I was fortunate. A friend of mine was an English major and wanted to get into editing. Since my first book was non-fiction, I didn't need anyone to evaluate plot or characters. The book just needs to flow and feel like a coherent piece. She was able to help me do that even though she didn't know the subject matter. She also did a copyedit pass later as the last thing before I put the book on the market.

Illustrations

As I was writing *Handbook*, I realized that there were several places where an illustration would be extremely helpful. I could hold my own using PowerPoint, but I couldn't do something that was to the quality needed for a book. I needed to find someone.

I poked around on some of the artist gig sites, but those always seemed a bit iffy to me. Lots of people were getting good work done, but trying to figure out who would do a good job for me was harder. Seeing examples of their work helped a bit, but nothing met my vision.

Fortunately, I had met a writer at GalaxyCon (K.M. Herkes, check out her *Rough Passages* series) that mentioned a good illustrator. She connected us; we did a phone interview, and a couple of sketches later, we were off to the races.

Since I have only worked with one illustrator, I can't say if this is typical. I provided a list of illustrations and he first provided a few hand sketches to set the direction. I would pick out the features I liked and then he would work it up in Illustrator and send it to me for feedback. Usually there was only one or two tweaks and it was good.

The interaction between the text and the illustration took a bit to work out. If an illustration is good, I needed fewer words to explain it. But you still need some words to introduce and explain the major points. Finding that balance was harder than I expected.

Know Your Audience

In non-fiction, more so than fiction, it is important to know your audience. So much of what and how you write will be determined by who you hope will read your work. You can't be totally wide (every single person on and off the planet!) and you can't be too narrow (left-handed, odd-day birthday, born in a town of 57 people, and speaks 14 different languages). You have to be somewhere in between.

When I started *Handbook*, I had a general idea of my audience: leaders in the Information Technology departments at manufacturing companies. One of the early pieces of feedback I received from my alpha readers was that the topics I was covering were not limited to IT departments at manufacturing companies. They could apply to all kinds of IT departments.

It was a lot of work to remove the manufacturing focus and add in other examples, but, in the end, it was worth it. The book now had a wider target audience.

Another problem I had to figure out was the experience of my readers. Some sections I had written to brand new IT leaders, other sections were written to those leaders with more experience. I wrestled with that for a week or two and decided to make *Handbook* for experienced IT leaders and write another book, *First Days*, for the new IT leader.

Once I had that figured out, the writing became easier. When I got stumped, I thought about what my target audience was and what they would want to know.

Writing Multiple Books at a Time

There are two schools of thought in the independent publishing world regarding writing multiple books at a time. I'm sure there's more, but I see them as two schools. Since one of my goals is to write multiple books, this issue interests me.

The first is to write and publish a book, including all editing passes, formatting, cover design, and upload it to the various sites. Then write and publish another one. This is how I did my first book. I had four editing passes: me, my outside readers, me again, and then my copyeditor. Then I did the formatting. Then I published it. Only after all that did I start the next book.

The second school of thought sees writing books as a pipeline. Maybe it is my manufacturing background, but this intrigues me. The idea goes like this. Write, let it sit (rest), self-edit, send out to editor (rest), format, cover design, publish. If you outsource the formatting and cover design, you might have additional rests. The trick is what you do during those rests in the process: work on the next book.

Established authors recommend letting your book sit before the first editing pass. Give your brain a break from that story. In addition, the outside editing will take time. Maybe you take a bit of promotion time before the actual publishing date to build awareness.

These are times when you can work on the next book. I am trying this by writing the first draft of this book (my third) while my second book is out at outside readers and my development editor. When I finish this draft, I will let it sit a bit while I go back and do another edit pass on my second book.

I don't have all the details worked out. I know I want to write multiple books and there seem to be parts of the process that would allow the overlap of two books. I'll let you know how it works out.

Chapter 6: Writing Fiction

Writing Fiction Is
A creative potpourri
I don't write for you, but me

Writing fiction is very different from writing non-fiction. There are different parts of your brain that are trying to do very different things. Non-fiction is about presenting facts and opinions in a way to teach or enlighten the reader. Fiction is about storytelling.

I realize the lines are getting blurrier and I'm not sure how I feel about that. Movies have long used the "based on a true story" caveat, which means that they got some ideas from the true story but then added a large dose of fiction to make it more entertaining. This blurs the line between fact and fiction and we don't always put in the time to make sure we know the difference.

On the other hand, there is also a class of non-fiction that has come out in the business world (and I presume other places) where a fictional story is written that illustrates the points that a non-fiction book would make. Some examples include *The Goal* (Eliyahu M. Goldratt and Jeff Cox)), *Gung-Ho* (Ken Blanchard and Sheldon Bowles), and *The Phoenix Project* (Gene Kim, Kevin Behr, and George Spafford). These books are written as novels with plots and characters and problems. But along the way, important business concepts are introduced and explained.

For now, I am viewing fiction and non-fiction as different things. While I was writing *Handbook* and *First Days*, I tried entering a few fiction contests with my short stories, and really struggled to switch mindsets between fiction and non-fiction. I finally decided to just keep the two worlds separate. You may have better luck than I did.

My fiction writing has been only short stories up to this point. I have written about twenty so far, some for contests, some as part of a class, and some just because.

What To Write

Write what you want to read.

My first draft of this book had that sentence as the entire chapter. I thought it said it all, but perhaps not. Shrug.

The two choices are "write what you want to read" and "writing to market." Writing to market means figuring out what people are going to buy and writing that. It works for some people, it doesn't work for others. As I am new to this writing thing, I don't think I know enough to write to market.

Perhaps you can add "write the stories you want to tell". This applies to fiction and non-fiction. If you have a story you need to tell, go for it.

But that easy answer doesn't help us in the beginning. We can hardly write a couple of paragraphs, much less a cohesive story. Where to start?

Descriptions, Dialogue, Characters, and Plot is where I started. You can find many books, podcasts, and websites on each topic and can spend all your retirement years just learning one of them. Here are some things that resonated with me.

Descriptions

Descriptions are one of the basic building blocks that underpin characters and plots. At the beginning, when you don't know what to write, describe something. A chair, a room, a tree, a car, a hamburger. Somewhere you went today, somewhere you have been, somewhere you want to go. Describe it in different ways. Sparse, flowery, long words, short words.

Remember to use different senses. Beginning writers tend to rely only on visual descriptions. I sure did. It was a blue chair. The carpet in the room was harvest gold. The car was old and dented. The hamburger arrived nestled in the tater tots. Think about all five senses. The squeak of the chair. The smell of the room. The touch of the tree. The taste of the hamburger. The smell of the tater tots. Mmmm, tater tots.

When writing descriptions, think of them as directing the attention of the reader. Don't write a long description about something that isn't important to the character, scene, or plot. Put another way, the longer the description, the more you are signaling to the reader that this is important.

As with everything in this chapter, you get better by practicing. If you have a daily routine, describe it. I wrote up arriving at work, from the parking lot to my start of work. If you have a favorite walk, describe it from memory and then add to it after the next time you go.

You have a lifetime of meals to draw on. Recall a favorite meal or meal time and write about it. What were the smells and flavors? What did it make you think about? Perhaps the memory had nothing to do with the specific food and everything to do with the meal (other people, location, situation). Write about that.

You have met so many people over the years. Describe a person you saw today or remember seeing years ago. Write a long version that might be at the start of a novel with that person as the main character. Write a short version where the person shows up briefly, but isn't important in the long run.

Describe your writing space. Describe a playground. Describe a physical object (a book, a table, a car) but imagine you are in a bad mood.

Write lots of descriptions to get a feel for your style. Write some descriptions that are not your style just to stretch your muscles. If you normally write short (like me), practice writing some longer descriptions. If your descriptions are normally longer, try writing a distilled version of something you have already written, capturing the essence of the description.

It is likely that during these exercises, you will get ideas for stories. Excellent. If a story wants to come out, let it. You can always move it from your practice document over to wherever you keep your stories. One of the surprising things I discovered was that my practice document became the source of new ideas down the road. When I went back and read some of my practice descriptions months later, there were some interesting ideas lurking in there.

Dialogue

"Dialogue is an important building block if you write fiction. Sometimes for non-fiction, too."

"Do I need to practice it?"

"Yup, just like everything else in writing."

"How do I do that?"

"I started with transcribing some brief conversations after they happened. I didn't worry about accuracy, I just did the best I could to see how it sounded when I read it out loud."

"Read it out loud?"

"Yeah, reading your dialogue out loud is a great way to make sure that it sounds the way you want it to."

"That makes sense."

"You can also practice by transcribing a scene from a favorite movie. This gives you a feel for what good dialogue looks like when written down."

"Isn't that plagiarism?"

"Not if it stays in your practice document. You are learning, not copying to use as your own."

"Ok, got some other examples?"

"Well, how about if two of your friends—that didn't know each other—met for the first time? Make up a place and reason and see where the dialogue takes you."

"You keep saying dialogue. Isn't it supposed to be dialog?"

"Those words sound the same to me."

"Umm, no. One version has a 'ue' on the end and the other doesn't. Which one are you using?"

"Does it matter? They sound the same."

"Not helpful, thanks."

"Anytime. Anyway, there are lots of dialogue possibilities. A blind date. People discussing where to go to lunch. A breakup scene. A person visiting a vet because their dog ate their favorite pair of Buzz Lightyear underwear."

"That was oddly specific."

"Yeah, never mind. The vet recovered them."

"Ew…"

"As. I. Was. Saying. You should work on emotions as well. Since you shouldn't tell your readers that a character is annoyed, you need to figure out how to show it in dialogue."

"Pfft, no, you can't. Now you are just lecturing me."

"Trust me, you can. You are retirement age, so that makes you old. That gives…"

"Wait, what? What did you just say? Did you just call *me* old? You are just as old as I am. In fact, I didn't exist until a few minutes ago when you made me up for this little charade!"

"Relax, I was just pointing out that you have a lot of experience interacting with real people and reading books and watching movies. Lean into that experience and use it."

"I've got something you can lean into. Calling me old…"

"Can we get back on track?"

"Don't go blaming me. You're the one writing this."

"Anyway, as I was saying. Emotions can come through the words without stating the emotions. Think of a time in your career where something went really well and write the dialogue as if you were explaining to a family member."

"Like that time I saved the company a ton of money and made the customer happy? That was so cool. I gotta bonus out of that. Bought a sweet new computer."

"Yeah, like that."

"I can do that."

"Remember last chapter when we talked about the Opponent?"

"Yes. I don't like my Opponent very much."

"Totally normal. You need to talk to your opponent to keep them out of your way. Write some dialogue between you and your Opponent where you set the rules. Remember that you are in charge."

"That's not a bad idea. Say, are we done with this dialogue bit? It feels kind of weird. You haven't given me a name or anything. I don't even know where we are or what we are doing while we talk."

"Pretty much, yeah. I didn't want to get into dialogue tags, setting, or the surrounding action because those come after the spoken words. My preference is to avoid them in the first draft. Write the dialogue so it is clear who is speaking, then add dialogue tags, descriptions, and actions."

"I noticed you also avoided saying anything about punctuation rules for dialogue. Isn't punctuation tricky?"

"No, not tricky. Just stupid. They set the rules way back when humans used lead type to prepare the printing plates and the physical size of the lead type for punctuation influenced the rules. Just learn them and follow them or else your editors get all twitchy."

"Ok, well, thanks. Can I go now?"

"Sure, have a nice day!"

"I don't know who I am or where I am, and I am pretty sure that I am a figment of your imagination. How can I have a good day?"

"Because I'm the writer and I decided you are going to have a good day."

"Got it. Guess I don't have much choice then."

"Nope."

Characters

Think about your favorite books or movies. They all have at least one character in the story that you enjoyed. Characters are why we care about a story. Doesn't matter if a character is good or bad or in the middle, they have to be interesting. The reader has to care about the character or else they won't care about your story.

That means that *you* have to care about your characters. And not just the main character, you have to care about the side characters as well.

In our years, we have met a lot of different people in lots of different situations. Think back to a few of the more memorable ones. What character traits do you remember? What physical traits stick in your memory?

In most stories, the characters change. They learn something about themselves. They learn something about the world. They learn something about the situation they think they are in. K.M. Weiland (highly recommended) talks about your main character's lie they tell themselves and how stories change the understanding of the lie.

I practiced by remembering old coworkers and created a story that would change their attitude. Now, in full disclosure, the story would change a trait that I found annoying into one I liked. One small way to deal with exasperating people. Shrug.

Sometimes characters don't change much. Think Jack Reacher or most of the Sherlock Holmes incarnations. They are the same character at the end of the story as at the beginning. The writers in these cases make the character interesting, make the recurring characters interesting (Watson is very different in most versions), and make the side characters in each story worth caring about. While the main character doesn't change much, the recurring characters and side characters do.

Here are a couple of other points about characters that make sense to me. Remember that I have not yet written a fiction novel, only short stories, and nothing published at this point. Once this book is out, I'll get into fiction and a future update will have more of what I learned.

- The amount of background work you do on each of your main characters depends on your style. Too little and your characters may not have the needed depth. Too much and you are not writing the story. Experiment with different techniques and see what works for you. Short stories are a good way to get better at characters.

- Everyone speaks differently. If there are no dialog tags, can you tell your characters apart?
- Different characters notice different things in the same setting. A foodie will notice different things in a restaurant than a carpenter. Write descriptions through the point-of-view character's eyes.
- Not every character needs a deep background. The bodyguard may be a real person, but if the story only needs them to stand there silently for part of one scene, there is no need to provide any other details.
- The Bechdel Test is a simple way to track if you are writing gender balanced stories. To pass, there must be (1) two or more female characters that, (2) talk to each other with no men around, (3) about something other than men, marriage, or babies. Note that the culture wars have expanded this test beyond its original intent. Keep it simple and don't overthink it. It is a quick mental check to make sure you have variety in your story. There are also, of course, the caveats about setting (for example, a monastery) or the total number of characters.

Plot

When you watch movies or shows, do you predict what will happen? Do you guess what will happen in the next chapter of the book you are reading? If so, you already have a sense of how plots go. Regardless of the genre, you have read or watched enough to know the basic structure of stories.

A lifetime of reading and watching TV and movies has built up a library of plots in your head and subconscious. You will be able to draw on and learn from this rich resource.

Pick a favorite movie or book. I'm sure you have a few that you have seen or read many times. Go through it and jot down the important plot points as you see them. Don't worry if you are "right" or not. This is about you learning, not about passing a test. Write down how the main character influences events at each point. Write down decisions. Write down changes in the character. Write down what you think is important.

Do it again. And again. Are there some commonalities to the plots? Are there types of events that resonate with you more than others?

If you have already done some research into storytelling, you have learned that there are many story structure books, articles, and techniques available. However, I found that until I did the above analysis on my own, I couldn't really understand what these techniques were trying to explain.

At this point in my career, I haven't used any of the templates (StoryGrid, Save The Cat, 3 Act, 5 Act, etc.) to write stories. But reading about them gave me (or at least my subconscious) a better sense of good storytelling. I am also not going to recommend a particular structure as I don't have the experience. It is worth reading about a few of them to know if it is something that will be helpful to you.

Some writers suggest using one of the story templates when it feels like your story is missing something. By mapping your story into one of the story templates, you may find the missing piece.

Trust your gut. You have been consuming stories your entire life and you know what you like. If you try to force your story into a formula that doesn't sit right, you won't like it.

Finish!

Ok, so this isn't an attribute of writing. But finishing is critical to writing and publishing a fiction piece.

Finish the work.
Finish the short story.
Finish the novel.

Finish the poem.

Finish the screenplay.

Your Opponent will fight hard to keep you from finishing anything. It will throw up obstacles, reasons, and emotions to keep you from finishing.

I think finishing is the most important part of the craft to learn. If you finish, you can put your work into the world and continue to get better. If you don't finish, it doesn't matter how great your characters or dialogue are, how moving your descriptions are, or how amazing your plots are. If you don't finish, no one will see your work.

I struggle with this. I have a novel and some stories that are not finished. But I have finished two non-fiction books and they are for sale. And if you are reading this, I now have three non-fiction books completed.

Two things influence my ability to finish.

First, all my jobs required that I finish tasks. Customer transactions had to be completed. Software had to ship. Projects had to finish. Regardless of what jobs you have had, you had to finish things. Sometime you were happy with the result, sometimes you weren't. Sometimes you worked really hard, and it didn't turn out well. Sometimes you slapped something together, and it turned out really well.

Second, we learned what *good enough* meant. It is a pretty high bar for some tasks (think medical devices). Other tasks didn't have to be perfect. Your story will never be perfect. The temptation to continue to perfect will be strong. There will always be a sentence that can be improved or a plot point to correct.

In the computer world, as soon as a software developer ships a new version of software, they know what they would do better if they got to do it again. This knowledge doesn't delay finishing, it informs their next project.

Same with writing. When you finish a story, you will have an idea about how it could be better. Those will help make future stories better.

Of course, I am not talking about shipping crap. But if you continually improve and set higher and higher expectations, the quality of your writing will improve. You will be able to finish better works in the same amount of time.

Striving for better is a fine and good thing—not finishing because the work is not perfect is madness.

> *Striving for better is a fine and good thing—not finishing because the work is not perfect is madness.*

Deciding that a work is finished is the second most important decision you can make in your writing. The first decision, of course, is to put in the work.

Like with all things, practice helps. In the short pieces you practice on, make an intentional decision to call it finished so we can move on to the next piece. Or have an end goal in mind. For example, write a short scene between two people playing cards, do one edit pass, and then consider it done. This may feel artificial, but the mindset of finishing is something to practice like the other skills.

Entering contests also helps. You must submit your work by the contest deadline or else you haven't entered.

Heinlein's Rules (see "Resources") addresses this directly. Rule #2 is "You must finish what you write." See Dean Wesley Smith's book *Heinlein's Rules: Five Simple Business Rules for Writing* for a deep explanation of these rules. Robert Heinlein was a prolific writer from the 1940s until the 1980s and knew a thing or two about finishing.

Finally, there is a quote, attributed to many people, about finishing. It says, "Art is never finished, only abandoned." I would replace the word "abandoned" with "released" but you get the point.

Learning how to finish your writing is as important as any craft technique.

Where Do Ideas Come From?

There is a ying-yang relationship between creativity and ideas. You can't have one without the other. You can't be creative without having ideas. You can't have ideas without being creative. Creativity is the engine, ideas are the output.

I mentioned earlier that you likely had to be creative during your career, regardless of your job. But that creativity is a different from writing fiction. Don't worry, it is not different like "I play soccer and now I want to learn tennis". It is more "I can cook but now I want to learn to bake bread". We don't have to learn a completely new skill, we just have to exercise our existing skills in a slightly different direction.

The creativity engine in each of us knows how to take everything we come across and combine it together into our internal compost pile. This is a remarkable part of our subconscious.

We were in our career long enough that we didn't really think about having ideas to solve problems or create something. Over our career, we had internalized much of the technology, domain knowledge, and prior work of others. This gave our subconscious a lot to work with, and the ideas come when we need them.

To be a fiction writer, there will be different inputs for us to internalize. Reading fiction, of course, is the primary way to do that, and we have been doing that our whole life. I have read a lot of fiction and seen a lot of fictional TV and movies. There have been good stories and bad stories. Stories that I want to revisit again and again because the characters are so compelling.

One question that writers frequently get asked in interviews or by new writers is, "Where do you get your ideas?" Some have useful answers, some have smartass answers, some say "I don't know."

The useful answers seem to fall into two camps.

- Pay attention to the world around you.
- The brain is a mysterious and wonderful thing.

Pay attention to the world around you

A good place to start is this quote. Card is an excellent writer with lots of styles in his writing.

> "Everybody walks past a thousand story ideas every day. The good writers are the ones who see five or six of them. Most people don't see any."
> — Orson Scott Card

As we go through our days, we experience a wide variety of people, situations, emotions, etc. The pandemic has curtailed things a bit, but remember, you have a lifetime of memories to draw on.

I started to keep a pocket journal and writing little snippets from my day. When I started, I was unsure of what to write. Should I write down only full ideas? Should I write plots and characters I thought of? Eventually I found my stride, jotting down short notes, usually ideas that popped into my head. Sometimes they were just a couple of words, sometimes they were a sentence or two.

I think this journal served two purposes. First, it got me paying attention to the stories around me. Second, when I looked back through the journal weeks or months later, I got more ideas from the notes I had taken.

I knew this from my work. In my career, I attended lots of meetings. So many meetings. In the useful ones, I took lots of notes. What I found was that I could recall the meeting very well, even if I didn't refer to my notes. The physical act of writing caused me to remember things better.

The journal does the same thing. It somehow emphasizes the things we choose to write down, and they get a little boost in our subconscious. The more I write down in the journal, the more the ideas seem to come.

I eventually moved to two journals. One, a small size I could carry easily. The other was a regular spiral-bound notebook where I could expand on ideas, keep track of my tasks for the day or the latest technique I learned. The small journal was just for ideas and the spiral notebook journal was my daily note taker and collector of ideas and tasks.

But what to write? Since real life is so rich with ideas, how can we pull out our "five or six of them"? I like to take a TV show or movie and swap out a character, setting, or plot point into something different. Or think of two very different things (character, character trait, etc.) and wonder what would happen if they existed together.

The brain is a mysterious and wonderful thing.
Earlier in this book, I mentioned the concept of the compost pile in our brain, specifically the subconscious. Compost piles take a strange mixture and turns it into fertile dirt. Kitchen scraps, food waste, yard waste, even those Brussel sprouts you keep trying to figure out how to cook so they don't taste like balls of sorrow and vinegar[1].

Stuff in. Fertile dirt out.

The same happens in our brains with everything in the world we come across. It all goes in and new stuff comes out. Through the mysteries of our brains, everything we put into them gets mixed together. Our creativity is just the natural result of everything composting.

I think this journal helped me be more intentional about putting fiction related stuff into the compost pile. The words didn't just end up in my journal — they also ended up being emphasized in my subconscious. The act of writing things down is just as important as having the words written for future reference.

---

[1] Yes, fine, you like Brussels sprouts, I get it. I don't, and this is my book. When you write your own book, you can make them the hero of your story. Hmmm... Brussels sprouts as a hero character... nope, I'm not gonna write that. You can have that idea.

To recap, pay attention to the world around you and jot down little notes to yourself to help feed your subconscious' compost pile.

Now I am sure that much of what is in my journal, especially at the beginning, wasn't very original. Not every idea is awesome. The goal is to set up a pipeline where ideas continually come out, allowing you to choose the ones that catch your interest.

Just like everything else, it is something you need to practice. Here are some other ideas I have tried.

> *The goal is to set up a pipeline where ideas continually come out, allowing you to choose the ones that catch your interest.*

- There are random character, plot, and setting generators on the internet. Pull one of each and write a short scene that ties them together. Don't worry if it is any good, just write.

- Take a character you know from TV or movies and write a scene where they meet someone in your life. Why are they meeting? Where? What happens?

- Enter contests that have a framework for the story. For example, NYC Midnight has several story contests every year where they assign you a character, a thing, and a genre and you have to write a short story. This year I got horror, an airman, and a scarf.

You will need to come up with lots of ideas to get one or two gems that you want to write about. If you only have one or two ideas, you don't really know if they are any good. If you have dozens of ideas, it is easier to tell which ones are worthy of taking forward.

As a last note on the topic of ideas, it is important to remember that, once you get your idea pipeline going, the harder part is writing the story using an idea. To oversimplify, eventually generating ideas will be easier than writing and finishing stories.

Chapter 7: The Tools

*Creative works will
Require good tools and knowledge
Learn to use them well*

If you are one to write on paper and never share with others, your tools are simple: a pencil or pen and paper. The right writing tool matters, as does the paper. However, if you are reading this book, you are likely going to be using a computer and software.

Computers and software? Those are my jam. To my friends' and relatives' chagrin, I can talk about them all day long. Let's look at some software tools that you might use.

Two major classes of tools are writing and formatting. Writing tools are for writing words. Formatting tools take your words and put them into a format used for selling, for example, ebook and print.

Writing tools can make it easy for you to plan with outline capabilities. They support moving sections of documents around for when you need to reorganize scenes, chapters, or sections. They allow you to type words easily, maybe supporting spell and grammar checking.

I learned early on that if I worry about formatting before I finish writing, the writing never gets finished. So I learned to put a hard line between writing (getting the words down) and formatting (fonts, pagination, chapter headers, etc.). For me, formatting is a distraction, sent by the Opponent, that prevents the

> *I learned early on that if I worry about formatting before I finish writing, the writing never gets finished.*

writing of words. I believe this is true for many people. It is likely true for you.

I used Microsoft Word heavily in my career. This tool combines writing and formatting. I would futz around with the document titles, headings and header/footer formats instead of actually getting the words down. In my career, the words were far more important than formatting, so I was wasting time on something that didn't matter.

When I became a writer, I felt that having a tool for writing and a separate tool for formatting would help me with that distraction. This helped me avoid the temptation to format when the writing got hard (hint: it always does at some point!). If the software I used had both writing and formatting, the Opponent would have another way to distract me.

You would use formatting tools if you independently publish your book. They take the words from your writing tool and lay them out on pages with margins and fonts and maybe pretty chapter headings. These tools will create the electronic files needed by the booksellers for printing and electronic distribution. If you have a traditional publishing contract, they will handle all the formatting.

Publishing tools are used to get your books into the sales channel. They require you to learn about metadata, pricing, geographic coverage, and getting paid. They are usually web-based, so you only need a browser. The ones that have costs usually have ways to publish for free (coupons or access codes).

Publishing tools can also include software to verify your ebook operates correctly on an eReader. Most channels for paperback and hardcover (KDP, IngramSpark) have tools that help you verify everything will print properly by showing you an electronic proof after you upload your files.

There will also be software you use for creating your website or interacting with social media. There will be small utilities you use for converting file formats.

Using software can be a double-edged sword. We have all been frustrated by software that didn't do what it was supposed to or didn't behave as we expected. Over my career, I have learned some software truths that make using software easier.

- Software is written by people. People aren't perfect. Software will never be perfect. There will always be bugs.

- Software that is used by lots of people and has a decent development team around it, is generally going to be fairly bug-free. If you have a problem, assume the problem is with what you are doing first, before claiming it to be a bug. For example, if you have weird behavior in Microsoft Word, I feel very confident saying it is your expectation of the software's behavior, not a bug. I am not saying that Word is bug-free (it isn't), just that the chance of you finding a true bug are very small.

- Software can be easy to use with limited features or have lots of features and be complex to use. Software that has lots of features and is easy to use doesn't exist.

- Free software may be free of cost, but with a few exceptions, most software that is free is getting something else from you, usually your name, email, etc. that is sold.

- Once you choose a piece of software to do something, you will use that software longer than any computer or phone you own. Which means that, someday, you will be moving the software, and any data files, to a new computer or phone. Check out how to do that before choosing a software.

- It is better to figure out how the developers designed the user interface than to expect that it works the way you want it to. Find software that fits your needs and accept the quirks.

The following sections will cover writing and formatting tools. I will provide some consideration to help you select a suitable tool for you. Note that software changes frequently and therefore any list I provide will not be comprehensive. Searching the internet is the best way to find all the currently available tools.

Writing Tools

When you start out, picking a writing tool will be driven by cost or by what you have access to. You may have a computer at home already and it probably has a word processor on it. Likely a general word processing tool like Microsoft Word, Google Docs, or Apple Pages.

At the beginning of your writing experience, the tools don't matter as much as just writing. Whatever tool you have is a fine tool. Just write.

Unfortunately, the tool that you have already on your computer probably handles both writing and formatting. Stay focused on the writing and don't do any formatting. The tool you already have probably has limited ability to help you organize or plot a book.

As you get closer to retirement, you may want to choose to move to a tool better suited to the writing life. Microsoft Word is a great tool for business use, but it isn't a great tool for writing a book. Having said that, a lot of books have been written using Microsoft Word, so you may feel differently.

So what should we look for in a writing tool?

- Lots of uncluttered screen to type our words. A busy user interface can distract from getting the words down.

- The ability to plan out your writing. If you are writing fiction, this may be plotting tools or places to keep notes on characters, story lines, etc.

- The ability to leave notes for yourself. As you are writing, you will think about things you want to remember to put elsewhere. For example, you may decide that one of your character's relatives needs some backstory. Making a quick note and getting back to your writing is better that scrolling back to early and typing in some of that backstory.

- An easy way to make backup copies. Any electronic file should be backed up regularly. Sometimes this can be done outside the writing tool, but having something inside is helpful. I think the best habit is to backup after each writing session and the tool should make it easy.
- The ability to handle longer documents. One problem with word processors is that they struggle on longer documents. A book that is several hundred pages long can choke the more common word processors.
- The ability to handle parts, chapters, scenes, etc.

I started out using Google Docs as I was already a Google user and had used it for other things. It is great as a blank canvas, but has the formatting distractions. Short pieces worked fine, but longer pieces did not.

For longer pieces, I had two choices. I could put everything in one document or I could break the piece into multiple files. Neither option was great.

One large document I was working on ran into some size problems with Google Docs that caused weird behavior. An internet search showed this was not uncommon. It was also difficult to move sections around if I decided that a different order worked better. Cutting and pasting long passages of text is risky regardless of the tool you are using.

I tried using multiple files, but the only organization tool available is folder names and filenames. A career in IT taught me that organizing using folder and file names is very limiting.

I don't remember where I came across Dabble, but I signed up and used it to write my two IT books and this book. While there are some formatting capabilities and more are getting added all the time, I view Dabble as a writing tool, not a formatting tool. The simple user interface makes it easy to focus on the writing without the distractions of formatting. Bold, italics, and quotes are available and that is sufficient for me.

Dabble runs on all platforms. This allowed me to continue working on my books on whatever computer I was sitting at as well as my phone when I had a few moments. All my writing is stored in Dabble's cloud and there is a backup feature that allows me to make a local copy after each writing session. This was easier for me than remembering to make backups of my computer.

At the time I started using Dabble, it was fairly new and had a single developer. Dabble has since grown and now has a development team with new features coming out regularly.

No matter what software you use for writing, consider switching how your display is mounted. Most computer displays are setup to be wider than tall. This is called *landscape* mode. Rotating the display 90° makes it *portrait* mode. You will need a special display stand for this. I prefer writing in portrait mode for one simple reason: more of my writing is on the screen at a time. I can get almost two full pages visible at a time and still keep the text large enough for my old eyes to read.

Formatting Tools

The words are done! The words are done! Time to celebrate a major accomplishment. Grab a favorite beverage, go to your favorite place, and do a favorite thing. Hopefully, dancing is involved.

Depending on the software you used for writing, you may or may not need new software to format. If you wrote in Microsoft Word or Google Docs, you can format in the same software. Otherwise, you likely need to change to make the book visually look like you want.

I intentionally chose a writing tool that doesn't do formatting. Formatting my book before I finished writing it felt like a distraction. The Instant Gratification Monkey loves formatting while writing. Writing is hard, and the Opponent uses formatting to distract us.

There is some formatting you have to do during writing. You need to have chapter and section or scene breaks. Fiction is usually straightforward as you really only need chapter and scene breaks.

You might have some major acts or parts that you want to organize the chapters into.

Non-fiction can be more complex. You might have pictures, illustrations, lists, or tables. Those can be hard to do in software focused exclusively on writing words. The writing software I used, Dabble, didn't support any of those things at the time. I had to use some tricks to mark my intentions around the words. But that kept me focused on the writing, so it was worth it.

When it came time to format *Handbook*, I worked with two options: Vellum and Adobe Indesign. I tried several products that were non-starters, but I won't list them as they may have gotten better since I tried them.

Vellum is focused solely on formatting a book, and really only fiction books. If you are formatting a fiction book, Vellum is very easy to use. Import your text, pick a style from a large set of options, and your book flows into the new format. I played with it using some of my practice stories and it worked pretty slick.

I ran into two problems with Vellum. First, Vellum runs only on a Mac and I work on PCs. There is a service called MacInCloud that gives you a virtual Mac. You log into MacInCloud's website and it displays your Mac user interface in a window on your computer. This can take some getting used to. That was workable, but the second problem was the showstopper. As it was a non-fiction book, I had illustrations, tables, and lots and lots of lists, both bulleted and numbered. Vellum didn't support that formatting.

I moved over to Adobe Indesign for my second attempt. The Adobe Creative Cloud is the industry standard for graphic artists. Photoshop is so well known for its ability to edit photos it has become a verb. Illustrator is the go-to software for non-photo graphics. InDesign is one of the major software products for laying out magazines, brochures, signs, and books. I had some familiarity with the Adobe products from a stint earlier in my career in the printing industry.

Learning new software was always enjoyable for me, so I dove in. InDesign has a large learning curve, so it isn't for the feint of heart. It falls on the "lots of features and complex to use" end of the software spectrum.

I had also used Microsoft Word extensively in my career to format documents to look nice when printed. This introduced me to concepts like styles, tables of contents, and fonts. These concepts moved over to InDesign nicely.

The internet was an excellent resource for learning InDesign. There were always several videos explaining how to do whatever I was trying to do. I didn't always get it right the first time, but I figured out everything needed to make the book look the way I wanted.

Remember where I strongly recommended that you finish your words before formatting? Yeah, that was from direct experience with my first book. I had gotten my second draft out to my readers, applied the edits and then moved it over to Indesign. This was a mistake. I had jumped too soon.

When I moved my manuscript to the formatting software, the master copy was no longer in my writing software. Turns out I still had a bunch of edits to do and now I had to do them in Indesign. Indesign is powerful layout software, but it is a terrible place to edit words.

One disadvantage of using separate software for formatting is that you now have to manage the primary version. If you make any edits to the text in your formatting software (and you will), the version in your writing software is now out of date. So when I go back and update *Handbook* for the next revision, I need to start with the InDesign version and not the Dabble version because the Dabble version does not have the text edits I made during formatting.

The editing process took me longer than it should have. This just emphasized the need to finish the writing part completely before starting formatting. When I wrote *First Days*, I did very little editing in InDesign and life was easier.

There is another class of formatting tools to consider. Each of the publishing sites (Amazon KDP, IngramSpark, Draft2Digital, etc.) has tools that will format your book. They work well for simple books and not all of them allow you to export to other publishing sites. If you are publishing on a single site and publishing a fiction book (which typically has simpler formatting needs), then look into these tools.

Consider physical size when formatting your paperback or hardcover. Choose the size based on genre and number of pages. Wander over to your local bookstore and browse the shelves with a tape measure to help you decide. I chose 6 inches by 9 inches for *Handbook*, and *First Days* will probably be similar as they are part of a series.

Formatting your book requires that you decide on fonts. If you are using a tool like Vellum or one of the publisher tools, you will have a limited set of fonts to choose from. Using InDesign opens it up to thousands of possible fonts. It is worth doing some research on font choices. Learn what *serif* and *sans serif* means and why it matters.

There is always the option of contracting out your formatting work. There are many people available to do book formatting if you don't want to do it yourself.

Look at books on your shelf or from the library. Start at the very first piece of paper and page through the book. You will see a title page, copyright page, forward, table of contents, introduction, and so forth. This is called the *front matter*. At the end, you might see an afterword, index, or other material, called the *back matter*. There will be a blank page or two at the end of the book.

These are all things that you will need to put into your book if you independently publish. Once you look at enough example books, you will get a sense of how you want to do yours.

Chapter 8: The Business

Selling your writing
Is a decision to make
Neither good nor bad

This chapter is for those that want to sell their writing and make money. Awesome. There is nothing wrong (and a lot right) with wanting to sell your work. I'm not planning on making a lot of money, but if I can cover my expenses and keep at it for a while, I'll be satisfied.

I'll focus mainly on books because that is what I am doing. Other writing (journalism, technical writing, marketing copy writer, etc) have other business issues that I don't know about.

I have learned something about books. I currently have two non-fiction books for sale. That was a big learning experience for me. I learned from others before me and made both good and bad decisions.

I strongly recommend reading Dean Wesley Smith's (see "Resources") book, *The Magic Bakery*. The premise is simple, but the lessons are many. Imagine you own a bakery. You sell pies. A customer walks in, selects a pie, buys it, and walks out with it. Here is the magic part: another pie, exactly like the first, appears. Ready for the next customer. That is copyright, book sales, and the long tail, all rolled into one magic money-making bakery. Those concepts are important if you want to make money from your writing.

The analogy is powerful and Smith explains it much better in his book. The first lesson for me is that I need to keep my copyright, my intellectual property (IP), no matter what (e.g., license the IP, don't give it away in any contract). And that by leveraging the IP, I can make more money from what I write. The second lesson is that, since the pie will magically stay available—no matter how many books you sell, people can buy more—the more I write, the larger and more appealing my bakery will be. Bakeries with more things to sell have a better chance of finding people who want to buy them.

There is a lot more to it, of course, than the simple description above, and I am still learning.

The books, podcasts, and internet articles I read provided good background on the business side of being an author. While the list of topics they covered was large, there seemed to be a few initial decisions I needed to make.

- Tradition or Independent publishing
- Amazon Exclusive or Wide
- Pen Names
- ISBNs
- Marketing
- Outsourcing

Traditional or Independent Publishing

There are two ways a writer can get published these days: traditional publishing and independent publishing.

Traditional Publishing

Traditional publishing refers to submitting your book idea or manuscript to a publisher. If they like it, they sign you to a contract, pay you an advance, and publish your book.

The publisher takes all the financial risks and does most of the work. The author writes the book and makes changes requested by the publisher's editors.

The author gets paid an advance. This is an advance on future royalties. If the author gets, say, $5,000 in advance, and the author royalty is $5/book, then the publisher has prepaid the author royalties for 1,000 books. The author will not see a royalty payment until the 1,001st book is sold.

Traditional publishers will also invest in marketing if the author already has an audience.

I consider traditional publishing to be a channel that has a high barrier to entry and they handle everything after that to get the book to market. The gatekeepers for the traditional publishers purchase only those books that they can sell at a profit. It can typically take a year or two from the time the contract is signed to the time the book is for sale.

One thing to be careful about when signing a traditional publishing contract is Intellectual Property (IP). Default contracts grant all of your IP to the publisher. Don't sign them. Only grant the minimum rights needed for that particular contract. This is an important area to learn about if you are writing fiction.

Independent Publishing(a.k.a. self-publishing)

The brief description of independent publishing is this: You do or pay for everything yourself. You have all the control. You have all the responsibility.

Independent publishing is a lot more work. You write the book like you do for traditional publishing. But you also have to find, hire, and use an editor. You format the book for printing or ebook. You are responsible for the book cover. You buy the ISBNs. You decide where the book should be for sale. You upload the files to the distribution web sites. You handle all the marketing.

I learned much about the business from Joanna Penn's *The Creative Penn* podcast. She is a strong proponent of independent publishing. She is not anti-traditional publishing; it just doesn't meet her goals for writing. Even then, she doesn't rule out a traditional publisher in her future.

I chose independent publishing

I went the independent publishing route because:

- Control. I wanted to decide what books of mine got published. I didn't want to submit manuscripts for approval. Maybe that was my opponent talking ("you'll never be good enough to get traditionally published!"). Sometimes you have to go around the Opponent.
- I love business. I've been in the for-profit business sector most of my career and enjoy all the different facets. Learning about the publishing business was interesting to me.
- I could do the work. A career of working with computers gave me the confidence that I can learn any software program I would need. A career in business gave me the confidence that I could figure out the money side.

Let's look at the two options a little deeper.

Independent Publishing	Traditional Publishing
No Gatekeepers	Gatekeepers
Financial Risk By Author	Financial Risk by Publisher
Author handles editing, cover design, formatting	Publisher handles editing, cover design, formatting
No Advance	Publisher pays advance
Author puts it into the channel	Publisher puts it into the channel
Author responsible for most marketing	Author responsible for most marketing

To me, it seemed like a trade-off between control and effort. Traditional publishing is less effort to get a book out, and you have less control over things like cover, markets, etc. Independent publishing gives you all the control and you have to do all the work.

Two things led me to choose independent publishing: gatekeeping and my love of business.

The act of proposing a book to a traditional publisher means they act as a gatekeeper. They may or may not accept your book. If they don't accept it, you need to change it and try again or go to a different publisher. Someone else is deciding if your book will see the light of day.

That isn't a bad thing. While this is becoming less true as time goes buy, there is a level of writing quality that this brings to the market. Many authors that get larger publishing contracts had early novels rejected. They often admit that the publishers were right in rejecting them because they weren't very good.

However, the thought of writing all those proposals and receiving all those rejections seemed overwhelming. I wanted to control what books of mine got published. I did not want to be at the mercy of a large publishing company.

My love of business also has led me to independent publishing. In my career, I have always liked the marketing and sales aspects of a company. I enjoy looking at the business from the top level, understanding how all the different pieces contribute to the business and financials.

Being an independent author means I would need to track all my expenses and decide about where to spend money. Book cover? Illustrations? Editing? Advertising? This interested me. I could spend all the time that I would spend querying traditional publishers to write and publish more books.

Amazon Exclusive or Wide

If you are in a large English-speaking country, chances are that Amazon is a major, if not the major, bookseller in your country. Amazon has a program that offers benefits if you sell your books exclusively through their program. This decision is basically about balancing the benefits of being exclusive to Amazon and selling to a wider audience.

Benefits of Amazon Exclusive

Kindle Direct Publishing (KDP) is Amazon's publishing arm. They were the first website to make it easy for people to publish and sell their own work at scale. This was great for authors and readers alike.

One of the current features of KDP is called KDP Select. This is a reading subscription service where the customer pays a monthly fee and can read anything in the KDP Select library. The author gets paid by how many pages get read. For certain genres like science fiction or urban fantasy, KDP Select can be very lucrative for authors.

The catch is that if you want to be in KDP Select, you have to be exclusive. You can't have your book available for sale anywhere else. You are 100% dependent on Amazon for all the revenue for that book. The exclusivity is renewed every 90 days, so it is easy to get out of.

Benefits of Wide

The term "Wide", as in "I am publishing my book Wide", refers to publishing everywhere, or at least more than just Amazon. Even though it may not seem like it, there are lots of other booksellers on the planet, both physical and online. In fact, if you look at both physical geography and population, Amazon is not the leader on most of the planet.

Amazon is the world's largest bookstore, but they aren't everywhere and there are millions of books being sold through other channels.

The choice is between being exclusive on KDP or publishing wide. KDP exclusivity may get you more money in the short term. Wide gets you to a larger audience that may get you more money in the long run.

I chose Wide

As my first book wasn't in one of the money-making genres at KDP Select, I chose to go Wide. I also didn't like the idea of totally depending on a single company for all of my writing business.

That doesn't mean that I ignore KDP. On the contrary, KDP is my largest seller with 90% of my sales, both paperback and ebook. But I have sales on other platforms I would not have if I were exclusive.

The decision between the two also depends on the genre. At this time, non-fiction doesn't do very well on KDP Select, but science fiction and fantasy does. Since my first books would be non-fiction, there was not much upside selling only on KDP Select.

However, when I move into fiction, I may choose Amazon exclusivity for short periods of time as I build up my library of books. The advantages of KDP Select for the genres I am interested in may make it worth it. While experienced authors strongly recommend not flipping back and forth between KDP Select and Wide, some have been successful moving once from KDP Select to Wide. I'll let you know how it goes.

Pen Names

Authors sometimes use pen names instead of their real names. Some reasons for doing this include:

- You have a common name and wish to distinguish your name from the others. This is especially true if you have a well-known name like Stephen King. People and algorithms will get confused and will react negatively, swamping the quality of your work.

- You don't want anyone else to know what you are writing. Perhaps you are writing a memoir you wish to keep from your family. Perhaps you have a job that won't look kindly on the writing you wish to do.

- You want to write in different genres and want to keep the bookseller's algorithms separate. For example, if you have written literary fiction and decide that you want to write a western, choosing a different author name allows the algorithms to fit the new book into westerns cleanly instead of shoehorning it back into the literary fiction category.

- Sometimes your first couple of books don't do well and you want a fresh start.

- You believe a name slanted towards a particular gender would help you. While this is becoming less of an issue than in the past and fewer people are doing it, it still happens.

- You have a long or hard-to-spell name that complicates your cover or makes it hard for people to find you in search engines.

Booksellers have long supported pen names. You will need to create an account using your real name so they can pay you royalties, but each book has a text field for you to enter the author's name.

Pen names impact the way Amazon works with their "Also Bought" and other part of their recommendation algorithms. If I used a single author name, it would recommend my fiction for non-fiction readers and vice versa. While this seems like a good idea on the surface, my understanding is that this cross-recommendation causes problems in the long run and your readers get confused and annoyed.

However, reasonable people can disagree with this, so check it out for yourself. One nice thing is that you can change it down the road. The publishing sites (Amazon, Draft2Digital, etc) check to make sure that the author's name matches what is on the cover. To change a pen name, update the cover and edit the metadata for your book.

The last thing I'll mention about pen names is this: if you get popular, your real name will come out. It always has and always will. In these days of the internet, fandom, and family will eventually figure out who you are.

I Chose Two Pen Names

I plan on writing both fiction and non-fiction. In order to keep the algorithms separate, I am using "John A. Bredesen" for my non-fiction and "John Bredesen" for my fiction. While not different from my real name, they are different names and technically are pen names. Of all these decisions, this one is one I think is the most likely to change someday.

ISBNs

An ISBN is a 13-digit unique identifier for your book. You likely are familiar with the barcodes that get scanned at the checkout register at a store. You may have heard of SKU (stock keeping unit) numbers. The barcode contains the SKU. These barcodes tell the computers exactly what product is being sold. Businesses manage their inventory using the SKU to uniquely refer to each distinct product. Think of ISBN numbers as SKUs for books.

Each format of a book gets a unique ISBN. For example, I published my first book as both a paperback and an ebook. This meant that I needed two ISBNs, one for each format, even though the book content was exactly the same. I expect to add hardcover and audiobook formats so that would be four ISBNs for that one book.

The International ISBN Agency defines ISBNs and licenses one organization per country to sell and manage individual ISBN numbers. Since it is per country and since there is one seller per country, the price ranges everywhere from free to very expensive depending on the country's opinion of people writing books. There is a web page to help you find the agency in your country that sells ISBNs.

Libraries require ISBNs, so if you want your books there, you need to get your own ISBN.

Some companies, for example IngramSpark and Draft2Digital, offer "free ISBNs" for books published exclusively through them. Similarly, Amazon offers a unique identifier called an ASIN (Amazon Standard Identification Number) and doesn't require an ISBN. These identifiers are only good for that company—you can't use them with other companies.

I Chose To Get My Own ISBNs

I bought my own ISBNs to give me the most control. They are expensive in the US in small quantities, but I wanted the freedom to sell my books where I chose to without worrying about different free ISBNs for different channels. I also want my books in libraries.

If limiting yourself to distribution through a single channel is what you wish to do, you don't need to worry about ISBNs. If you wish to publish through other channels, that is, if you want to publish *wide*, you will need to buy ISBNs.

ISBNs are expensive compared to other costs of publishing, but the cost goes down as you buy more. My first ISBN purchase was a ten-pack because I figured I could commit to two books. It also turned out that I need four ISBNs per book because I intend to (someday) publish a hardcover and audiobook version of both *Handbook* and *First Days*. So, I will need to buy more for this book. Since this writing thing seems to be working for me, I will probably buy a larger pack of ISBNs, which will dramatically drop the price per ISBN.

Book Cover Design

Book covers are important to our book's success. Think about how you buy books. You probably have entered a search term on a bookseller site and scanned through the list of books. You also have wandered through a bookstore, looking at the shelves and pulling out books that looked interesting. Because humans are very visual, it is likely that you scanned through the thumbnails or the physical covers to see what grabs your attention. This scan is all about the book cover.

The old saying about not judging a book by the cover was said by someone who doesn't understand how books are actually sold. Yes, I know, and agree with the fact, that outward appearances can be deceiving for everything, including books. But in the book market where there are tens of millions of books, people judge books by the cover all the time. Whether or not we like it, the visual cover plays a large role in how readers find our books.

The best, and most common, advice I came across was to look at the other books in the section of the bookstore (online or physical) where your book would reside. Think carefully about how your cover will look next to the others.

My first two books would never be in physical bookstores because I aimed them at a tiny audience (leaders of the IT department) so my focus was on how it looked in the online stores. I spent a lot of time looking at the covers of the books in the categories my books would be in. When I had some drafts of the cover, I took a screenshot of the Amazon category with all the books listed and insert my cover to see how it looked next to the other.

I wanted it to look like it belonged with the other titles and have a little something that made it pop. This is very easy to say and hard to do unless you are working with an experienced book cover designer. Whether or not I succeeded is up to others to decide.

You will need a different cover for each format of your book. While the general look will be the same, each platform has their own requirements for covers. If you have a paperback and are selling through KDP and IngramSpark, the cover format requirements are slightly different between the two.

Ebooks only require a front cover, but the requirements are yet again different from paperback. Hardcover are different from paperbacks, especially if you do a paper sleeve for the cover. Audiobooks are square and are never printed.

So it appeared that I would need seven different versions of the cover if I published in all formats I was thinking about.

1. Paperback - KDP
2. Paperback - IngramSpark
3. Ebook - KDP
4. Ebook - Draft2Digital
5. Hardcover - KDP
6. Hardcover - IngramSpark
7. Audiobook

Because I did the book design for *Handbook* myself, I struggled. The platforms have software that verifies the cover meets the requirements, and it took me a while to get past that check. The error messages weren't great so there was a lot of trial and error before I got it right. I still can't say for sure what I did to make it work.

For *First Days*, I am working with a cover designer and have had a much easier experience. This all just reinforces that independent publishing requires either time or money to do all the work that traditional publishers handle.

Making Your Book Available to the World

You have finished writing and formatting your book. Congrats! I hope you take a few moments to do a happy dance for yourself. You have finished the hard part. The step of publishing it to the world is much easier than writing it.

However, *easier* doesn't mean *easy*.

Getting your book out into the world takes a bit of work that will feel very far away from writing words. Software and systems will frustrate you and you will yell at your computer at least once[2].

I won't be able to provide you with the 'simple path' through it all because there isn't one. All I can do is cover some of the big decisions you will need to make and explain what I did, both successful and not.

Putting it out into the world means that people can buy it through their local physical bookstore and online through Kobo, Apple books, Google Play books, Amazon, and a host of others. One eye-opening learning for me was the number of online ebook sellers on the planet. My reading experience was with the one big company in my country, but they aren't the primary book seller in most of the countries on the planet.

Go to https://books2read.com/IT-Leaders-Handbook to see all the places people can buy *Handbook*. Note that this doesn't in-

---

[2] Even those of us that are comfortable with computers yell at them. Except we are yelling at the people that built them because we know they could have done it better.

clude the thousands of bookstores that order from Ingram, which is fed by IngramSpark.

After doing a bunch of reading, here is what I decided to do for my first book. I likely will change this as time goes by and the industry changes.

For paperback (and eventually hardback), I chose to go through IngramSpark and Amazon KDP (Kindle Direct Publishing). For ebook, I went directly to Google Play and Amazon KDP. I used Draft2Digital to get to Apple Books, Barnes & Noble, Baker & Taylor, several library services like Hoopla, Overdrive, and Bibliotheca, and subscription reading services like Scribd. I also used Kobo for distribution into a larger range of countries than Amazon provided.

Ingram is a worldwide printing and distribution company. Most physical bookstores around the planet can tap into Ingram's catalog and order physical books. IngramSpark is their website service that supports independent authors.

Amazon is the largest bookseller in my country, and several others, but they are fairly isolated. If you put your book up on Amazon KDP, it will only be for sale on Amazon. Bookstores won't order from Amazon and libraries effectively can't.

I used Draft2Digital and Kobo to cover as wide a range of possibilities. There is a tradeoff between going to the dozens (hundreds?) of ebooksellers directly or using these two companies to cover as much as possible. As both are expanding their reach, it seemed like a good balance between my time and the size of the distribution channel.

Whether you are going through only one distributor or many, the steps are generally the same.

1. Get an account on the distributer's website.

2. Create the book by entering title, description, author name, and the rest of your book's metadata.

3. Upload the inside of the book.

4. Upload the cover.

5. Review online proof.

6. Set pricing and other distribution settings.

7. Click publish.

After a short delay (a few hours to a few days) for technical quality checking, your book is for sale. If you are like me, you will immediately buy a copy for yourself to prove that you did everything right. This is especially true for printed versions.

It is also very cool, and very normal, to want a printed copy on your shelf. In fact, it is so expected that Amazon and IngramSpark allow for purchase of author copies at a discounted price.

When you upload your cover and content of the book, most distributers will run a check on them to make sure that they are technically correct. This ensures the print book will print correctly and look good and your ebook will look good and operate correctly on eReaders. They won't find typos or other content problems, though.

Unfortunately, you will need several versions of your cover and contents to match the requirements of the different platforms. Make sure you have a good naming convention to keep all this straight.

One more tip: using bookmarks in your browser, set up a group of tabs to display your book on all the different platforms. It will help with checking to make sure everything looks ok (which you should do once in a while). But, more importantly, it is seriously cool to open all those tabs at once and see your book for sale on all these platforms all over the world.

So now you have your book out there for the world to buy. Now we just have to let the world know.

Book Description & Metadata

Selling books online requires metadata. Metadata is data *about* your book and includes title, description, author name, publisher, ISBN, categories, and many others.

The title is the most important piece of metadata. When browsing, people will use the cover and title to make snap judgements about a book. Do our eyes skim over it on the screen or bookstore shelf? Does it capture our attention?

The description is the next most important piece of metadata. It is used in the online stores where their search engines will use the description to match words the reader is searching for. It will also show up on the back of your paperback and hardcover versions. Think about wandering through the bookstore. You may pick a book up by the cover and title, but the first thing you do is flip it over and read the back cover description.

Knowing the audience is important for writing the book. It is equally critical for writing the book description used in selling and marketing your book. The description needs to be laser focused on the target audience.

Unfortunately, I can't provide a simple set of steps and rules for writing a book description. I did all the internet searches and read lots of articles. They helped, but I don't feel that I understand the art of the description well enough to provide guidance.

The only takeaway that seems right to me is this: The description's goal is not to tell people about the book, its goal is to get people to buy the book. It is a tease, not an explanation. It should make people want to know more about the characters, setting, or plot.

If the book is non-fiction, the description should communicate what the reader will learn or what problem the book will help the reader solve.

The description sets expectations, especially for genre books like science fiction, romance, western, etc. If a reader buys a book and it is not what they expected, they will be more upset than if your book is not very good.

As we did for book covers, look at a lot of examples. Wander through the section of a bookstore you think your book will sit in and look at other descriptions. Look at the best sellers in that area to see their descriptions. Look at a lot of books and ask yourself if you want to buy this book. If so, what specifically was it about the description that caught your attention and intrigued you.

Marketing

One brutal reality that both traditionally published and independent authors mention is the fact that authors need to do their own marketing. Only the largest names in the book business, like Stephen King, Neil Gaiman, Dean Koontz, etc. will have significant marketing dollars thrown at their books by someone else.

If you are a first-time author picked up by a traditional publisher, it is unlikely there will be much marketing money for your book. The publisher expects you to build your own audience. In fact, there are some indications that having or not having an audience will influence if they offer you a publishing contract.

So I realized fairly early on that I was going to need to do marketing myself. I wasn't thrilled with this, but if I wanted to sell books, I didn't have much choice. The days of writing the book, tossing it over the publisher, and moving on to the next book are long gone.

Marketing is about making potential readers aware of your book and connecting them to the places they can buy it. In other words, awareness and where to purchase (a.k.a. channels).

The starting point is to know where your readers currently buy their books. What channels are they buying from? Amazon is currently the largest bookstore, but it is a long way from being the only one, especially if you look at the entire planet. Many people also get their books from libraries. Reading subscriptions (Scribd, Kobo Plus, and Amazon Kindle Unlimited) are becoming more popular with more added each month. Authors get paid from these subscription services by the number of pages read, not by the number of books sold.

Each of these channels will have a royalty. This is the payment you get for selling your book on that channel. For selling books, it can range from 35% to 70% depending on the price of the book and the channel you choose. Do your research as these things change frequently.

Some genres are very popular on Kindle Unlimited. For example, at this writing, urban fantasy writers would do well to look hard at Kindle Unlimited (even with the exclusivity limitation). That takes you to the Amazon Kindle Unlimited exclusivity versus going Wide decision I talked about earlier in this chapter.

Once you decide what channels will sell your book, you need to get potential readers to be aware of it.

To be clear, I am very early in my book marketing journey. There is much to learn and everything is changing so quickly that it feels impossible to keep up.

Marketing lessons that make sense to me

There is a ton of information available on the internet and in bookstores about how to market your book. I've read enough to make my head swim, but here are a few things that make sense to me.

Content Marketing: For non-fiction, like my first two books, content marketing is a strong technique. Content marketing means using the content of your book as a marketing tool. At first glance, this may seem confusing. Give away the content of my book in order to sell my book? I admit I struggled with the concept when I first heard about it.

The concept is to take small bite-sized pieces of your content and put them out in a place where your potential readers can find them, usually social media and a personal website. Choose small points and concepts from your writing. No need to do a full chapter (unless you have small chapters).

Joanna Penn is a master of this with her non-fiction. She has a podcast and a website where you can find the content of her non-fiction books. But she still sells lots of books because people want the convenience of the book.

Content marketing is a little different for fiction. The authors that use this technique typically provide short stories set in the same world, perhaps using the same characters as the larger books. The concept is to give the reader something useful or interesting for free in exchange for connecting with you.

By sharing your content, you show potential readers that you know what you are talking about. You show them your writing style. You give them something for free that is valuable to them. If they get value from you, they are on their way to buying a book from you.

> *What I did: I used the content marketing heavily for Handbook. I took pieces of changes and write blog posts. Scheduled once a week, these posts were short 1-2 minute reads that provide some useful ideas for IT leaders. I scheduled the topics out for months and then kept them posting. It seemed to work as the number of readers increased.*

<u>It takes time.</u> Your book will be on the market for years. It is very rare for new books to get a major spike, especially from a new author. No matter what you do with your first book, it is extremely likely that you will only sell a few copies in the first months. We have to build an audience for our writing and that takes time.

Maybe you strike it hot on your first book and it does well. Great! That's fantastic. But you can't count on that happening.

Plan on the long run.

> *What I did: There really wasn't anything specific I did on this other than lower my expectations for sales of the first book. Reminding myself that this book would be on sale for years help keep things in perspective.*

<u>Write more books.</u> If you are only interesting in writing your one book, say a memoir, disregard this one. If you are writing fiction and want to have a bit of a career as a writer, then write more books. Experienced independent publishers say that, when you are just starting out, the best time and money you can spend on marketing is to write the next book. Having multiple books out increases the chances that a potential reader will find you.

> What I did: About four months after I released Handbook, I started working on First Days, my second IT book. As soon as I sent First Days off to the editor, I started on this book. When these two books are on the market, I intend to switch over to fiction.

<u>1,000 true fans:</u> I came across a concept of "1,000 true fans". If you have 1,000 true fans, and enough books written, you can make a decent living. Here is one of the articles that laid the groundwork of this idea: https://kk.org/thetechnium/1000-true-fans/.

Some background first. The starting points for this concept are as follows.

- The world is a large place, currently containing 7+ billion people, speaking many languages in many cultures.
- The rise of the ebook makes it easier to sell globally. An ebook is available to anyone on the planet with a device and access to the internet.
- Mass market success is becoming a disappearing phenomenon. With a few exceptions, there are very few books or movies that sell large numbers as in the past. There are so many books and movies available, making it harder to break through to mass market success.
- Independent publishing allows the author to capture more of each sale (e.g., higher royalties).
- Books never go out of print and can be for sale longer than our life spans.
- Technology has allowed the independent author to move faster than a publishing house can.

The 1,000 Fans concept is straightforward. By finding those people that like your work, and continuing to put out work they enjoy, you can make a decent living.

Just because the concept is straightforward doesn't mean that it's easy. It isn't. Finding the 1,000 is hard. Writing enough books to keep those thousand readers interested is hard.

Figure out what kind of reader will like your books and put the effort into finding them. This focused approach, so the theory goes, will work better than marketing to the entire world. Figure out where they hang out online or in person and put your marketing efforts there.

> *What I Did: The IT Leaders I was aiming for with my first book are very comfortable hanging out online. I focused on LinkedIn and a few IT online communities. I made sure that I was posting regularly about things other than my book and constructively commenting on other's posts. I tried creating a mailing list for IT leaders but I haven't had much luck yet in getting people to sign up. I think part of that is I haven't sent out newsletters to the mailing list. That takes time and energy and I think I will continue to put that elsewhere. Maybe I will do a newsletter when I get to fiction, but, for now, I don't think I will do a newsletter for non-fiction.*

<u>Try one thing at a time.</u> The correct approach to fixing computer problems is to only change one thing at a time and then see if the problem has gone away. That way you know what specifically fixed the problem. If you try more than one thing at a time, you don't really know what fixed the problem.

Marketing has the same phenomenon. If you try multiple things at one, you may not know the specific benefits of each attempt. Try one thing at a time and measure how well it worked. Then try something else and see how that works. Don't try a bunch of things all at once, especially at the beginning when you are learning new techniques.

As you get more experience, you learn what works and what doesn't. This allows you to combine tactics. When you release, for example, your fourth book, you would do everything that has been successful in past releases.

> *What I Did: I took this concept to heart on advertising. I started out using Amazon ads for Handbook. I ran the automated keyword ads for a couple of months to see how they went. Then I turned off the automated keyword campaign and turned on a manual keyword campaign, using what I had learned. After that had settled down, I tried turning off ads to see if there was an organic search market for my book. If I could sell a few books each month with no ad spend — and do that for years — that would be ok.*

<u>Anonymity is more of a threat than piracy.</u> New writers sometimes worry about having their work stolen. The fear of posting on the internet, the fear of sending it to an editor, the fear of sharing it with a writing group, the fear of content marketing. What if someone steals it and publishes it under their own name?

This is 100% the Opponent throwing this into their head to keep the writing from ever seeing the light of day. The fear of someone stealing their writing keeps them from moving forward.

Sure, there is a small chance this will happen, but it is far more likely to happen to established authors than to a new writer.

The greater threat to a new writer is anonymity. Far more writers fail because no one ever learns who they are or hears about their book than fail due to having their work stolen.

The copyright law is clear, the instant you put the words down on paper or your computer, you own the copyright. Dates on your computer files or in the writing systems you use help establish that if you need it.

If you really feel strongly, you can also take the step of registering your copyright with your country's copyright office when you publish it. It is usually low cost and may help down the road if you become famous.

> *What I did: I used content marketing for my non-fiction and am not worried about anyone stealing my content. When I get to fiction, my plan is to promote and give away free short stories to build an audience.*

Have your own website. There are lots of companies that support author pages. You can make your home on any of the social media platforms. The risk is that they will change and no longer be ideal for you. The priorities of these platforms is to make money, not help you succeed. Sure, if they can help you make money, they may make more money in some vague, indirect way. But do you really want your career to depend on a single company?

John Scalzi (see "Resources") points out that having your own website, while more work, keeps you from depending on large tech companies that can change their algorithms whenever they want and don't really care about the individual.

> *What I did: I have my author-name website (johnbredesen.com as well as a site for my IT books (the-it-director.com). I used WordPress to create it so I can move it to whatever hosting service I want. I'm not sure that this has been more work. Figuring out Facebook business pages isn't easy either. Most of my posts are on my sites, but I do post on social media on LinkedIn, Facebook, and Twitter.*

Advertising

Sigh. Advertising. The thing we all love and hate at the same time. We love Super Bowl commercials or the annual British Commercial winners. We hate the fact that they are everywhere. We love it when an ad is for exactly something we are looking for and hate the privacy issues around that level of detailed tracking. We dislike ads that have nothing to do with us. We like ads when they are clever.

We have been experiencing ads our entire lives. Estimates range from thousands to tens of thousands per year, depending on the job we have. You probably have some ads stuck in your head that you remember at odd times.

Selling books requires advertising. I don't think there is an alternative as effective as running ads, at least at the beginning. Even if you are using the content marketing concept, you need to get people's attention. The next alternative to advertising is to build your own mailing list, which isn't much easier.

I didn't want to wait until I had several books to advertise. My first book was an IT book and would only be interesting to a small niche of people. I also wanted to learn some about advertising to help me in the future.

As Amazon was the biggest book selling platform for English books, I tried Amazon Ads first.

Amazons Ads work in two ways. They use keywords to match with people's search terms. Also, they figure out who might like your book based on other books they have purchased. This second way also uses keywords, so getting keywords right is the key.

They have an automatic setting where Amazon algorithms figure out the keywords for your book. They take your book title and description, build an initial set of keywords, and then refine it from actual use. There is an option for you to set your own keywords.

The first month, I spent far more on ads than I got in sales. I expected this, but it was still painful as I was spending all of my royalties on ads. Recently, I have turned off ads on my first book to see what happens. Time will tell.

> *What I did: I did both. I ran the automatic ad campaign for two months and then used the resulting list of effective keywords as the starting point for my manual keyword list. I then eliminated keywords that were getting clicks, but not sales.*

Your Author's Website

When I decided I needed a website, I poked around a little to see what was available. I had used Wix on a project for my wife and it was ok, not great. This was a long time ago so I'm sure it is better.

WordPress kept popping up as a tool people were using.

There are actually two different "WordPress" entities that you need to keep straight.

WordPress is an open-source website software. At the time of this writing, it is the most popular software used to create both personal and business websites. CNN and Forbes and other big name websites use WordPress. If you use WordPress, you need to configure servers and backend software and do all the work yourself, but you have an amazing amount of control.

WordPress.com (note the ".com" at the end) is a website hosting company, meaning they take all the WordPress software, package it up into a service you pay a monthly (or annual) fee, and keep it running so you don't have to worry about the techy part. You still have to design your website or hire out to one of many WordPress consultants that are available.

> *What I did: I chose WordPress.com for my website. It is a platform with the largest number of people who know it and the largest amount of internet resources, classes, and support.*

Karma in your author business

I believe in karma.

Karma is one of those fluffy, hard to define words. It gets used by serious religions, new age proponents, and internet memes. I tried to look up a definition and gave up after the first five paragraphs of the Wikipedia page.

That's ok, I have my own definition and here is it is.

> *The world sucks. The world is wonderful. If I put good actions and thoughts into the world, it, or at least my little corner, will suck a little less. I want to live in a less-sucky world.*

This isn't a mathematical thing where my doing a good deed leads specifically to some improvement. This is a general "be nice, try to do more good than bad, and help people out where you can" kind of thing. In the podcast Freakonomics, Stephen Dubner signs off with the statement, "Take care of yourself, and, if you can, someone else." I love that.

This is also something that isn't dependent on others. It is just me. When life sucks, it is very hard to do this. Sometimes it is impossible. I think of it as something to strive for, knowing that I won't be able to do it all the time.

So how does this relate to a writing career?

In any career, experts recommend making connections. But most of us have no clue how to do this. Here are some ideas.

Find an author you like, get on their mailing list, volunteer to be a beta reader. Make sure you do the work and provide good feedback quickly. Don't look for anything in return.

If they have a community online, join in. Be a positive contributor. Don't look for anything in return.

The most important aspect of karma, at least for me) is that you should never expect anything in return. If you hold a door open for someone with an armload of packages, you shouldn't expect a thank you. You did something nice for someone and that is the point. You can't look at it as a transaction where both of you get something.

As you make connections in the writing world, this is especially true. People can often smell someone who wants something a mile away. Doing things for others because you want to and expecting nothing in return is the right way.

I can't stress this enough. You need to do good for others with no expectation of getting something in return. Of course, you will learn about the writing business, but that comes from paying attention, not someone doing something for you.

Some people have difficulty with this. I understand that. It doesn't feel good when the person with the packages doesn't say thank you. My irrational pet peeve is when I let someone into my lane in heavy traffic and they don't give me a wave.

To be clear, I am not talking about work transactions where you hire someone to perform a task for you. They are called transactions for a reason. Both sides do something that helps the other. I pay the illustrator money and they create a book cover for me. I pay an editor and they make suggestions for how to improve the book.

Karma is squishy and there is a lot to argue about in what I have written above.

But I believe that karma is real.

Summary

After Retirement
Enjoy the Writing Journey
Be nice to yourself

I've covered a lot in this book, but here are the main ideas I want you to take away.

- Becoming a writer at retirement gives you the benefit of a lifetime of experience, perspective, and self-awareness.
- The Opponent is your biggest challenge. Understand what it is and have a plan for dealing with it.
- Enjoy the writing process itself. If you do, it won't matter how many books you sell.
- When selecting what to write about — things like genre, subject, topics, characters, etc. — write for yourself, not anyone else. If you like what you wrote, it's good. If you don't, learn how to make it better next time. Make sure it isn't your Opponent making the good/bad call.
- Formatting is separate from writing. Use tools to stay focused on the writing. Do not worry about fonts, pagination, chapter headings, etc. until *after* the book is written.
- Teach yourself to write clean copy the first time through. Keep spelling and grammar checkers turned on and fix things as you go. If possible, fix it yourself instead of relying on the checker to fix it. Like a baseball player fielding hun-

dreds of ground balls to build that skill, practice will reduce your common mistakes.

- Your brain works faster than your fingers. It is worth some effort to speed up your typing speed.
- Writing every day (or as many days as you can) is really important at the beginning. Put the time in to get better. Put some intentional planning into this writing so you are either working towards finishing a piece or practicing a skill you wish to improve.
- Waiting for the muse to strike is a bad plan. Get your butt in the chair and write. It will make it easier for the muse to find you.
- Heinlein's Rules.
- Be kind to yourself. Be compassionate to yourself. Society has put the tortured artist model in our head. There is no reason you need to buy into it.

The transition from a full-time job in a career to becoming a writer is a journey of faith. Faith that you are capable. Faith that you can manage your life to make it possible. Faith that you will eventually write something you are proud of.

Faith in yourself.

The Opponent will try to make it about what others think and will try to get you to quit. The Opponent will try to distract you and keep your focus away from writing.

At the end of the day, you have to decide if this is something you want to do. Is it a dream? A hope? Or is it something that you want enough to make a plan?

You read this book, so you are putting some effort into it. Whether or not you become a writer, I hope you find whatever path is right for you.

Good Luck!

Resources

The taste of new skills
Some easy some with struggle
Each as a journey

Learning something new, especially something that I want to learn, is always exciting for me. My typical technique is to look for those that are successful in the field and start learning how they talk and think about the topic.

For a topic like writing, this meant finding the authors that I like and seeing what they said about learning to write. I looked for common patterns that show up with different writers. I looked for the big decisions I would need to make.

Variety is the key here. There is no one book, website, or podcast with all the answers. Reading or listening widely will expose you to lots of different thoughts and approaches. You can make up your own mind about what feels right to you. A lot of what you read won't make sense or will feel overwhelming. That's ok, keep reading, keep listening, make your plan by taking small steps and small risks.

The first resource I found was the writing podcast called *Writing Excuses*. Episodes came out weekly, were about fifteen minutes long, and there were many years of episodes already published. Perfect. I started listening to it on my commute.

The second important piece I discovered was The Creative Penn, the business name of Joanna Penn. Her website, her podcast of the same name, and a handful of writing books, are a gold mine of information. She has documented her entire writing career (she started in 2008, the early days of independent publishing) in books, podcasts, and web articles. Her podcast contains interviews with many others in the independent publishing field, which led me to other podcasts and books.

Over time, a couple of resources showed up again and again.

- *Turning Pro* and *The War of Art* by Stephen Pressfield. He has a few other books on writing and creativity that are worth reading as well. These books are not for the faint of heart. His belief is that being an artist is really hard, but mainly because of ourselves, not the world around us. We need to get out of our own way, work our butts off, and stop whining. If you view yourself as a victim of the world and have no wish to change, these are not books for you.

- *On Writing: A Memoir of the Craft* by Stephen King. As the author of many books, and many turned into movies, King is clearly a successful writer. Half-memoir and half-craft, this book presents his view of writing. Everything from habits to grammar. It isn't a long book and worth the read. One of his interesting points is about rejections. Submitting a story and being rejected can be devastating, especially if you give too much control to the Opponent. King turned all this on its head by turning it into a game. How many rejection slips could he collect? His thinking was that if he got a rejection slip, it meant he had tried something. The fact that he failed (was rejected) was less important than the fact that he was doing something. He viewed submitting as the win and the acceptance or rejection as secondary. Some writers have taken this further and set a goal for rejections. "My goal is twenty-five rejections this year." That forces them to submit at least twenty-five times. When something they wrote gets accepted, it is a magnificent surprise.

- "Heinlein's Rules" by two people. Robert Heinlein , one of science fiction's first masters, put them down in an obscure article. They are so short, I can reproduce them here:

1. You must write.
2. You must finish what you start.
3. You must refrain from rewriting except to editorial order.
4. You must put it on the market.
5. You must keep it on the market until sold.

Dean Wesley Smith expanded on these rules with his book *Heinlein's Rules: Five Simple Business Rules for Writing*. I'll say more about Smith in a moment. These rules come from the same place as King's rejections. If we want to write, we must write and submit. Written before the independent publishing revolution, putting it on the market means submitting it to someone for publication. As you can see by rule #3, Heinlein was not a "polish until perfect" kind of writer. He knew you have to finish the piece and only change if the editor asks for changes, after they bought the piece.

For me, the power of Heinlein's rules is in #2: You must finish what you start. It has been tempting to give up on something or switch over to a more interesting project. I have done this several times and have work to do before I can live this rule. I know that whatever rationalization I use for not finishing comes from my Opponent. It may have a germ of truth in it, but if I don't finish the work, there is a decent chance I will never go back to it and no one will ever see it. And the Opponent would win again.

- National Novel Writing Month (NaNoWriMo) Every November, thousands of writers sit down and try to write 50,000 words for their novel. The non-profit NaNoWriMo organization has lots of resources for writers. The thinking is that this commitment ("I'm doing NaNoWriMo this year to write 50,000 words for my novel") helps people get the words written. There is a community aspect to NaNoWriMo that helps many. Some people love it and have eventually published the book they started during the month.

Some people think it is a waste of time because, well, the Opponent throws out lots of reasons. I think that, like everything else I am telling you, indeed like every other piece of writing advice, it is merely one more option for you to think about. I have done NaNoWriMo every year since I have heard about it. I have never hit 50,000 words. But I consider those three Novembers to be successful.

The first one was early in my writing days. I was practicing and trying to get my daily word count higher. My fingers were often the slow part. I had a hard time typing fast enough to keep up with my brain. Before November, I could write 200-400 words/day. During that month, I was able to hit 1,000 words/day multiple times the last two weeks, and I even had a 2,000 word day. NaNoWriMo helped me figure out how to write lots of words. With the habits I developed during NaNoWriMo, I have been able to sustain 1,000 word/day while still working at a job.

I used my second NaNoWriMo to write four short stories, one per week. I wasn't aiming for word count; I was aiming for story count. I had three story ideas planned, but I intentionally kept the one week completely open to see if I could make up a story on the spot. Again, the month was successful. I came out of it with four stories, two that I submitted. One has become a longer piece that is still in my to-be-written pile. One of them, I'm sad to say, I let the Opponent win, and it is sitting ignored on my hard drive.

I used my third NaNoWriMo as an incentive to write this book. It turns out my prior book (the second overall) needed a push to finish my edits and get it to my editor. So I used the end of October as my deadline for the other work, allowing me to focus on this book in November. I didn't make 50,000 words, but I was thrilled with my progress.

The trick to getting the most out of NaNoWriMo is to make the goal be your own. If I do another NaNoWriMo, it will be because I have a goal that fits into the month, not because I want a NaNoWriMo badge. Make the goal your own. Want to write 50,000 words for a novel? Great. Want to speed up your typing or get more short stories written? Great. The month should be about your goals and your writing. Use NaNoWriMo as a tool, not an end. It isn't a win if you never look back at those 50,000 words. It is a win if you write 10,000 words that were exactly what you were hoping for.

The following are some people that have been influential in my thinking about becoming a writer. They are in no particular order. Some are repeats from above but included because people bounce around when reading these types of books. None of these people are perfect, indeed they will be the first to tell you that. None of the advice will work 100% for you. They are a good cross-section of suggestions, viewpoints, and "how I did it" that I found useful.

There are many others that I have learned from, but listing everyone would be the same as an internet search for "how to be a writer."

John Scalzi

Scalzi is a major author in the science fiction space. He has had an online presence for years and is a good example of creating an online community. As you look at it, remember that he has been doing it for years.

Stephen King

King's part-memoir, part-writing instruction book *On Writing* was the first book I read on writing. The memoir portion was interesting, but the writing was eye-opening. Having read other books since then, I don't know that I would put it at the top of the list, but I recommend this book to help get started.

Robert Heinlein

Heinlein was one of the original science fiction best-selling author. I have read and enjoyed many of his books and short stories, but that isn't why he is on this list. He wrote a short article in a writing magazine that has reverberated widely through the (not just science fiction) writing community over the years. "Heinlein's

Rules" are still the best way for someone to approach getting published. Dean Wesley Smith's book, *Heinlein's Rules: Five Simple Business Rules for Writing*, provides the proper context for the rules in today's world.

Tim Urban

Urban has a useful and hilarious TED Talk about procrastination that I highly recommend. Many of the posts on his website are interesting but aren't related to writing. If you have ever procrastinated (and all of us have), the fifteen minutes of this TED Talk are worth your time.

Stephen Pressfield

Writer of fiction (*The Legend of Bagger Vance*, *Killing Rommel*, and others) and non-fiction (*The War of Art* and *Turning Pro*). His non-fiction has helped me understand that becoming a writer is not for the faint of heart. If I wanted to do it, I had to be serious about it. I couldn't just dip my toe in the water and call it good.

Dean Wesley Smith

New York Times and USA Today bestselling author of over 200 novels and hundreds of short stories. He has influenced me in several areas.

(1) His book called *The Magic Bakery* which covers how authors should think about their work if they want to be in the business of selling their writing.

(2) Smith is a massively prolific writer, publishing over a million words of fiction. As he repeatedly gets on bestseller lists, I think he has kept his quality up. His thoughts on prolific writing (write clean, repeatedly cycle through thousand word chunks) have influenced the habits I am trying to build.

(3) In his book, "Writing Into The Dark", Smith talks a lot about "trusting yourself." With all the books, TV, and movies we have consumed over the years, we know what "stories" are and what works for us. We don't have to spend lots of time learning all

sorts of templates and methods to learn what a good story is. We already know.

Joanna Penn

Massive website and over 500 podcast episodes chronicling her writing journey. Tons of resources, opinions, and connections to others in the field. If you listen to one writing podcast, this should be it.

From her website: *Joanna Penn is an award-nominated, New York Times and USA Today bestselling author of thrillers under J.F. Penn and also writes non-fiction for authors. She's also a podcaster and an award-winning creative entrepreneur. Her site, TheCreativePenn.com has been voted in the Top 100 sites for writers by Writer's Digest.*

Neil Gaiman

Gaiman is an English author of short fiction, novels, comic books, graphic novels, nonfiction, audio theatre, and films. He has a Masterclass (masterclass.com) that is very helpful for fiction writing.

Daved G. Driscoll

I've known Driscoll for years, and we have had many rollicking conversations about art, being an artist, and creativity. He firmly believes that every human has creativity hard-wired in. Unfortunately, the creative spark is often under the blanket of adulthood and we need to work to bring it back. His thoughts on this topic have been a large contributor to my self-confidence as I start this journey.

Elizabeth Gilbert

Gilbert wrote *Eat, Pray, Love* and other books. I highly recommend her book, *Big Magic*. She focuses on curiosity, not passion. Compassion, not regiment. Like Daved Driscoll and Dean Wesley Smith, she explains how creativity is inside each of us, we just need to pay attention to it and give it space to grow.

K.M. Weiland

Weiland writes both fiction and non-fiction. Her non-fiction site, and podcasts, have an immense amount of information about the craft of writing. Browse her article list and you will find something helpful.

Here is other podcasts and websites I have found useful.

Podcasts

- Writing Excuses
- The Creative Penn Podcast for Writers
- Six Figure Authors
- Writers, Ink
- Ann Kroeker: Writing Coach
- Helping Writers Become Authors
- Alliance of Independent Authors: AskAlli: Self-Publishing Advice
- The Self-Publishing Show
- #AmWriting
- Stark Reflections on Writing and Publishing
- Fiction Writing Made Easy
- The Self-Publish Strong Podcast
- Freakonomic: What's so great about Retirement?

Websites & Organizations

- Writes Digest
- Alliance of Independent Authors
- NYC Midnight (contests)
- Indie Author

Author's Notes

Thanks for reading! I hope this book is useful to your future as a writer. I am having a grand time writing as I got a head start the last few years at my "day job".

I intend to update this book after a few more years of experience so if you are interested, sign up for my email list at johnbredesen.com. I don't send out a lot of emails, but I will keep you posted on upcoming book releases. And, hopefully, entertain you a bit.

This book was both easy and hard to write. Some sections, like the business section, were straight-forward. Others, like the Opponent and Spouse/Partner section, were really challenging. Putting those thoughts down required a lot of thinking about what I really believe.

In the end, writing this book helped clarify, for me, what this writing journey looks like. They say that every book changes the author and that is certainly true for this one.

I hope you write and finish the book(s) you want to write. They will change you. Good luck!

Acknowledgments

No one writes and publishes in a complete vacuum. I am grateful for the others that have helped me along the way.

- Ex-Libris II Writers Group. Their encouragement and feedback helped me at the start and have kept me going. The group's fearless leader is Bonnie Geisert Way and the members are Aaron Brunache, Harold Way, Cynthia Mauleón, Kate Norlander, and Peju Solarin.

- My editor Kristin Erlandsen keeps challenging me to write better. I have a tendency to disagree with many of the standard writing rules. Kristin makes sure that I at least understand the rules and makes sure that I have a good reason to break them. Any broken rules in the book remaining in the book are the result of my stubbornness, not Kristin's editing.

- I want to thank several folks who are retiring or have retired and picked up writing. I put out a call to learn about what others think about this transition and several responded. I am grateful for their input. This includes Mark Tomlinson, Linzi Day, Bryce Wilby, and several who wish to remain anonymous.

- And as always, my magnificent wife Joyce supports me through all (ok, most of) my wild ideas. She has supported this whole writing idea from the beginning and I am grateful for that. Thanks Sunshine!

Book Writing Notes

- **Start2Finish:** Six months
- **Tools:** Dabble Writer, MS-Word, Adobe InDesign, ePub testing apps (Kindle Previewer, Nook, Kobo Books)
- **Soundtrack:** Envy of None (1st album), Taylor Swift (shuffle), Beethoven's 9th, Rush (shuffle), Samantha Fish (shuffle), Styx (Crash Of The Crown), The Warning (Mayday), Jethro Tull (The Zealot's Gene)
- **Availability:** Wide (many physical & ebook bookstores around the planet) books2read.com/Writing-Into-the-Sunset
- **Learn More:** johnbredesen.com

Author Bio

John Bredesen has gray hair, laugh lines, and has recently retired. After working in academics and business for his adult life, he is entering retirement, specifically to become a writer. John lives in Minnesota, USA with his marvelous and tolerant wife and a dog much smaller than he ever thought he would own. He also can be found at campgrounds around the country.

John has two other books available (*The I.T. Leaders' Handbook* and *The I.T. Leader's First Days*). These are books aimed at the Information Technology leaders in all industries.

You can find him blathering semi-regularly at john-bredesen.com.

Publisher Information

Kennd

Kennd Publishing is a US company based in Minnesota. Kennd publishes both fiction and non-fiction books that expand your horizons. For more information, visit https://kennd-publishing.com/ or email info@kennd-publishing.com.

Other Books by John A. Bredesen

The I.T. Leaders' Handbook, John A. Bredesen, 2020
If you are an Information Technology (IT) manager, director, or CIO, this book will help you raise your game. Starting with foundations such as change management, technical debt, and categorizing the work, the book builds to cover important aspects of Business, People, and how to think about the ever-changing Technology IT needs to deal with.

The I.T. Leader's First Days, John A. Bredesen, 2021
Every leader starts out somewhere, and this book helps the new IT leader start strong. IT starts with basic skills than an IT leader needs and covers what the leader should do in their first few months on the job. The second half of the book is a distill and rewritten version of the Foundations, Business, People, and Technology sections from *The I.T. Leaders' Handbook*.

Index

A

Apple Pages 102
audience 11, 48, 49, 50, 75, 77, 81, 111, 113, 114, 119, 123, 124, 126, 130

B

book sales 55, 109

C

Community 48
Continuous Improvement 59, 60

D

Dabble 34, 103, 104, 105, 106, 153
Daved G. Driscoll 29, 145
Dean Wesley Smith 93, 109, 141, 144, 145
Draft2Digital 106, 116, 117, 119, 121

E

Elizabeth Gilbert 27, 32, 54, 145

F

formatting 38, 52, 82, 99, 100, 101, 102, 103, 104, 105, 106, 107, 120

G

Google Docs 102, 103, 104

H

habits 4, 24, 29, 31, 34, 65, 66, 140, 142, 144
Heinlein's Rules 93, 136, 140, 141, 143, 144

I

imposter syndrome 24, 28
Indesign 105, 106
IngramSpark 100, 106, 117, 119, 121, 122

J

Joanna Penn 73, 111, 125, 139, 145
John Scalzi 130, 143

K

karma 133, 134
KDP 100, 106, 114, 115, 119, 121
K.M. Weiland 89, 146

M

Malcolm Gladwell 4
Microsoft Word 100, 101, 102, 104, 106
Mozarts 55

N

NaNoWriMo 141, 142, 143
National Novel Writing Month 141
Neil Gaiman 124, 145

O

Opponent 25, 26, 27, 28, 29, 30, 31, 32, 33, 34, 35, 36, 37, 40, 48, 50, 59, 60, 73, 76, 77, 87, 88, 92, 99, 100, 104, 112, 129, 135, 136, 140, 141, 142, 149

P

partners 63

R

retirement age 3, 20, 23, 28, 38, 61, 87
Robert Heinlein 93, 140, 143

S

Signal-to-Noise 11
spouse 63, 64, 65
Stephen King 4, 115, 124, 140, 143
Stephen Pressfield 26, 140, 144

T

Tim Urban 26, 144
Typing speed 63

V

Vellum 105, 107

W

Writing Excuses 12, 61, 75, 139, 146
writing talent 55, 56

www.ingramcontent.com/pod-product-compliance
Lightning Source LLC
Chambersburg PA
CBHW072055110526
44590CB00018B/3176